THE COLLECTION

by Liz McGrath

COOKBOOK

Photography by Craig Fraser

To my cooking daughters

THE COLLECTION

by Liz McGrath

COOKBOOK

My grateful thanks to Craig Fraser and Petal Palmer. We had so much creative fun together!
Also to Joy Clack, Jane Last and all my patient chefs in the three hotels.

First published in 2003 by
Struik Publishers
(a division of New Holland Publishing (South Africa) (Pty) Ltd)
Cornelis Struik House
80 McKenzie Street
Cape Town 8001

www.struik.co.za

New Holland Publishing
is a member of the Johnnic Publishing Group

2 4 6 8 10 9 7 5 3 1

Publishing Manager: Linda de Villiers
Editor: Joy Clack
Designer: Petal Palmer
Photographer: Craig Fraser,
with the exception of pages 6, 8–12, 14, 15, 16 (bottom left)
and centre of foldouts – photographers unknown
Stylist: Petal Palmer

Reproduction by Hirt & Carter Cape (Pty) Ltd
Printed and bound by Sing Cheong Printing Company Limited

ISBN 1 86872 842 0

Log on to our photographic website
www.imagesofafrica.co.za for an African experience

CONTENTS

6
Foreword

8
Introduction

The Cellars-Hohenort   The Plettenberg   The Marine

17
The Greenhouse

65
Sand at
The Plettenberg

97
Pavilion at
The Marine

41
The Cape Malay
Restaurant

127
Seafood at The Marine

151
The Basics

163
Index

Foreword

One of the most exciting and rewarding moments in my life as a hotelier was being invited to join the Relais & Chateaux organization and, strangely enough, the request to produce this cookbook ranks up there alongside it.

Ever since I can remember, food has played an important part in my life. I grew up in England and my mother's cooking was superb, simple and beautifully presented. My father, who was born in Russia, was a gourmet with exquisite taste, and the whole family always discussed the merits of good food around the dinner table.

Cooking came naturally to me – I never remember having a lesson – and I was lucky enough to marry a man who was equally interested in food. Each year we enjoyed a holiday that revolved around culinary activities, invariably visiting Relais & Chateaux hotels in France and sampling delicious *haute cuisine* prepared by Michelin-star chefs. Today I continue this tradition to keep abreast of the latest cooking trends, and to exchange ideas with Relais & Chateaux hoteliers worldwide is always an inspiration.

Our three children followed in our footsteps from an early age and conversation and critiques on cooking have always been part of the family meal. I'm also lucky enough to have grandchildren who like nothing better than to sit around my large table in Johannesburg, where a traditional Sunday lunch is the norm.

Enjoying good food and striving for excellence in the kitchen has been with me most of my life, and when I became a hotelier the culinary side of the business was very important. Although not professionally trained, I believe my knowledge of food is a great asset in the running of The Collection's five restaurants. I truly enjoy being involved in the hotel kitchens, discussing the finer details of the menu with the chefs and, on many occasions, helping out during service.

Today, most of the world's five-star hotels boast a specialist restaurant, often run by a famous chef. The Connaught and Claridges in London, under the umbrella of Michelin-star celebrity chef Gordon Ramsay, are perfect examples. Here in South Africa, our chefs have not yet reached celebrity status, but we have such amazing talent that I'm sure South Africa will soon achieve wider recognition in the world for its gifted chefs and unique cuisine.

One of my greatest pleasures is to see young people, often without formal training like myself, advance within the restaurant and hotel industry, which can take them anywhere in the world. Hopefully they will return to our wonderful shores, with greater experience and the knowledge that the grass is not greener on the other side. I take great pleasure in watching my 'protégés' blossom and prosper wherever they are. But I am particularly proud when they do so in South Africa, serving spectacular dishes created from our sensational fresh produce.

LIZ McGRATH

INTRODUCTION

A seagull drifts in for a dip in
The Plettenberg's pool, which seems
to merge with the ocean beyond.

There is a collection of three hotels in the beautiful Western Cape Province of South Africa that is extraordinarily special. The hotels are small and elegant and welcome guests like valued friends. To stay at The Cellars-Hohenort in Constantia, Cape Town, The Marine at Hermanus and The Plettenberg at Plettenberg Bay, and to eat at their tables, is a quintessential experience for serious food lovers. The hotels are, in essence, the antidote to modern mass tourism, and together they are known as The Collection by Liz McGrath.

Each hotel has been embraced into the exclusive Relais & Chateaux, which promotes the Five Cs – courtesy, charm, character, calm and cuisine. They fit perfectly within this prestigious group of independent hotels, which boasts only 10 other members in South Africa.

What makes The Collection so special, however, is that these hotels have been created, nurtured and sustained by owner Liz McGrath, an extraordinary woman with impeccable taste and a true sense of style.

Liz McGrath is a dynamic perfectionist with a natural flair for interior design and a sharp nose for superb property in stunning locations. With her late husband Gerald, a powerful figure in the recording industry, she had a lifetime's experience visiting the world's best hotels and restaurants and rubbing shoulders with the international showbiz set. Today, she's lauded as one of the world's premier businesswomen by a host of organizations including *Fortune* magazine, IBM and the Veuve Cliquot champagne house.

Liz has had to search for chefs who shared her philosophy that classical dishes should be simplified, allowing the flavour of fine South African produce to speak for itself. She understands that chefs want to produce food that is unusual, individual and often complex, but she firmly believes that nothing compares to a perfectly cooked piece of meat or fish, expertly handled and beautifully presented. The chefs that she has discovered and developed are among the best in South Africa, and she works closely with them, testing every recipe before it appears on the menu.

The legendary view from The Plettenberg across Formosa Bay.

9

Summertime at The Plettenberg,
with the sweep of Formosa Bay
as a backdrop.

THE PLETTENBERG, PLETTENBERG BAY

In the beginning, before Liz McGrath imagined that she would become a world-class hotelier, she and her husband bought the one-star Look-Out Hotel in Plettenberg Bay. Their plan was to build a family home on the site, which boasts a breathtaking view.

After the death of her husband, Liz decided to turn the decrepit Look-Out into a small, exclusive hotel. She knew, after all, what it was like to stay in a Relais & Chateaux-style hotel, now she had to learn how to run one.

Liz opened The Plettenberg in 1987, and within 18 months the hotel was invited into the fold and boasted the Relais & Chateaux gold fleur-de-lis. And with well-earned reason. The Plettenberg is a joy, with its sun lounge lit by old brass ships' lamps and the winter lounge heated by a traditional log fire. Built atop a rocky headland, the magnificent vistas of sea, mountains and golden sands add to the tranquil luxury of this exclusive hotel.

Sand at The Plettenberg

Headed up by Executive Chef Christiaan Campbell, the restaurant serves modern South African cuisine, with The Collection's customary emphasis on fresh seafood and local produce. There are summer vegetables, asparagus and herbs from the nearby farms, crayfish, prawns, oysters and line fish straight from the sea, and succulent lamb from the Little Karoo. For those with a sweet tooth, the gratin of passion fruit mousse, trio of sorbets and chocolate tart with chocolate sorbet are all irresistible.

Diners who can drag themselves away from the restaurant with views that extend over the pool terrace and across the sweep of the bay to the mountains beyond, can alternatively book to eat in the hotel's wine cellar. The terracotta-tiled vault houses more than 4 000 bottles of South Africa's best wines, but there's just room for a candlelit table for two.

BELOW LEFT: The interior of Sand at The Plettenberg, where exquisite dining awaits every guest

BELOW: The earthy tones and natural shades add to the restaurant's ambience

THE CELLARS-HOHENORT, CONSTANTIA

This handsome property sits on the eastern slope of Table Mountain, surrounded by verdant gardens, manicured lawns and woodland, 300-year-old Chinese camphor trees, huge oaks and indigenous yellowwoods. Dating back to 1693, the estate was once the home of Hendrik ten Damme, chief surgeon of the Dutch East India Company and even today, with its polished wood floors and log fires, grand piano and bookshelves filled with Cape histories, it is more like a gracious home than a hotel.

With its duck pond, bluebell wood, tennis court and views from the veranda over its own vines to False Bay beyond, this is the hotel Liz McGrath never meant to buy. She simply fell in love with the property, once the wine cellar for the Klaasenbosch Estate, and bought it in 1991.

She had already transformed it into an elegant 30-bedroom, five-star hotel when the old Spilhaus family home next door, dating back to 1907 and known as The Hohenort Manor House, came up for sale. Unable to resist, Liz restored it to its original design and replanted the same variety of grapes that had previously grown here for centuries. Now it also boasts a traditional herb parterre, a canal flanked with white iceberg roses and petunias, two pools surrounded by cerise-coloured bougainvillea, a Gary Player-designed putting green and a small *boules* pitch.

The Greenhouse

With its floor-to-ceiling plate-glass windows overlooking the lush gardens on one side, and glass doors leading onto the terrace on the other side, this restaurant is aptly named.

At lunchtime the atmosphere is contemporary, light and airy, while after dark it is transformed into cosy, candlelit sophistication.

At The Cellars-Hohenort, food and wine is taken very seriously. General Manager Fredrik Aspegrén is not only a trained chef, but also chairman of the Relais & Chateaux Association of Southern Africa, and an active member of the International Wine and Food Society. In addition to the fine food created by Executive Chef Phil Alcock, The Greenhouse offers one of the best wine lists in the country, along with a fully qualified French sommelier, Tatiana Marcetteau, to advise which wine would best complement each course.

The Cape Malay Restaurant

Liz has a great appreciation for South Africa's Cape Malay cooking. She believes it is one of the world's most interesting cuisines, all too often overlooked by chefs who are star-struck by European cooking and who ignore the unique spicy flavours on their own doorstep.

Cape Malay cooking combines the original foods of the Khoisan people, the spices introduced from Indonesia and the cooking skills of indentured labourers and Dutch settlers alike, refined over 300 years into a unique culinary tradition.

It was after meeting Chef Cass Abrahams, the aficionado of Cape Malay eating who has inspired its renaissance, that Liz first had the idea of starting a restaurant dedicated to this cuisine.

The subtle, Malay-influenced décor and mellow candlelight enhance the authenticity of this restaurant, where the food is expertly prepared by Head Chef Martha Williams. The hot towels soaked in rose water encourage diners to eat some of the dishes with their fingers and enjoy the relaxed atmosphere.

The hotel gardens provide the backdrop for The Greenhouse (top), with its fine cuisine created by Executive Chef Phil Alcock (centre). Right: The cosy interior of The Cape Malay Restaurant.

THE MARINE, HERMANUS

Perched on top of the cliffs at Hermanus, The Marine enjoys one of the southern hemisphere's most spectacular seascapes. As early as late May and peaking from October to December, the hotel also delights visitors with views of humpback and southern right whales, which migrate to these waters to calve and nurse their young. And to witness the world's best land-based whale-watching, here you don't even have to get out of bed!

Built in 1903, with no electricity or running water in the bedrooms but in an era when London doctors would send their wealthy, convalescing patients to South Africa or to the Cape to take the healthy 'champagne air' of Hermanus, The Marine soon became a fashionable hideaway for English gentry.

This was another hotel Liz McGrath didn't mean to buy – until she popped in for tea in March 1998 and was captivated by the idea of restoring the decaying building with its multi-million-dollar location. By October of that same year, The Marine had 45 individually decorated bedrooms, a heated pool, a beauty spa and two restaurants.

BELOW: The welcoming pool in the enclosed courtyard at The Marine (bottom).

The atmosphere is pure luxury. Sea-blue-and-white bedrooms boast four-poster beds and idyllic views, while downstairs in the orangery, cane sofas with deep cream cushions face huge arched windows that overlook the Atlantic Ocean. Outside, guests sip chilled sparkling wine and enjoy lunch at the pool, enclosed in a courtyard garden with walls clad in flowering bougainvillea.

The Pavilion at The Marine

Apart from the food created by Head Chef Louis van Reenen, the star of this lovely restaurant is the ocean itself. Here diners enjoy the dramatic panorama of the Shipwreck Coast and Cape of Storms and, from May to December, the antics and aquabatics of the whales just below in Walker Bay.

As dusk falls over The Pavilion, the mountains disappear, the sea and sky turn swiftly black and the arched windows reflect the romantic glow of candles in the rich cream dining room with its well-stocked, glass-walled wine store in the centre.

There may be a hint of the Mediterranean in the ambience here, but the food is pure South African, using the fresh fruits of the land and sea. Gourmet evenings are held regularly, when a master wine-maker from a local vineyard will muse on the best vintages between courses.

Seafood at The Marine

This restaurant epitomizes contemporary cool with its menu of ocean-fresh fish and fruits de mer, and the kitchen theatre is a controlled frenzy of activity as Chef Rumé Booysens and her team prepare their dishes under the diners' gaze.

The cold waters of the Atlantic abound with Cape salmon and tuna, snoek and steenbras, red Roman, kabeljou (kob) and many other line fish. And each day guests can partake of this bounty – from seafood soup to grilled Walker Bay sole.

Liz McGrath's personal signature is stamped on the character of each of her hotels and restaurants, along with a strong feminine influence. It's a passion, she says, to make people feel welcome, as if they're coming into a home. But she refuses to admit to having a favourite restaurant among her Collection. It would be like choosing between your children, she says, and each is very different. After tasting some of these recipes, perhaps you can judge for yourself.

BELOW: The freshest fish and seafood are served daily, always expertly prepared and beautifully presented.

BOTTOM RIGHT: Diners can watch the organized chaos of the kitchen at the Seafood at The Marine.

THE CELLARS-HOHENORT

★ ★ ★ ★ ★

the Greenhouse

The Greenhouse epitomizes Liz McGrath's exceptional style. The décor is up to the minute and tranquillity and simplicity are the key.

Guests can choose to dine either out on the restaurant's terrace, or in the conservatory, with its spectacular view of Table Mountain. And the most talked-about round table in Cape Town rewards diners with sweeping views over one of the city's most beautiful gardens.

The large plate-glass windows highlight the 300-year-old camphor trees alongside some rare species of ferns and indigenous plants, and a spectacular old oak tree is enclosed in an atrium within The Greenhouse itself.

The eclectic menu offers a range of flavours, tastes and experiences and its award-winning wine list, arguably one of the largest in South Africa, features a selection of the finest Cape wines.

PHILIP ALCOCK – **Executive Chef**

Philip has trained in some of Europe's finest kitchens with their top celebrity chefs. From a flying start at the elegant Moulin de l'Abbaye in the French Dordogne, to the Michelin-star Le Auberge de Grenouillére in northern France, he returned to his native England to work under Marco Pierre White at Quo Vadis, where attention to detail and flavour are paramount and simplicity rules.

Philip moved to the famed Le Manoir aux Quat'Saison, Raymond Blanc's Michelin-star hotel near Oxford. As Head Chef at Le Petit Blanc, Philip worked closely with Raymond on the recipes and menus for his restaurants, heading a brigade of 22 chefs and gaining invaluable experience, expertise and inspiration.

After a trip to Thailand, where he studied the flavours and methods of Thai cuisine, Philip was finally lured to South Africa to become Executive Chef at The Cellars-Hohenort.

Philip is passionate about the flavour of his food, and describes his style as contemporary classical, with the emphasis on simple, clean tastes using the best of local and organic produce.

Butternut *soup*

This is a velvety smooth soup, great for cold nights and with just enough spice to heat things up a little.

20 ml vegetable oil
500 g butternut, diced
1 large onion, chopped
10 ml grated fresh root ginger
2.5 ml chopped chilli
5 ml salt
2 litres vegetable stock
   (see recipe, page 153)
a handful fresh coriander stalks
salt and freshly ground black
   pepper to taste

(see recipe, page 153)

CROÛTONS

6 slices white bread
50 g butter

GARNISH

fresh coriander leaves
diced tomato

SERVES 8

The soup Heat the oil in a large pan and gently sweat the butternut and onion for 5 minutes. Add the remaining ingredients, except the pepper, and slowly bring to the boil. Reduce the heat and simmer gently until the butternut is soft. Place in a blender and blend to a smooth purée. Season.

The croûtons Remove the crusts and dice the bread into 1 cm cubes. Melt the butter in a frying pan and gently fry the croûtons until golden brown. Remove and drain the excess butter on kitchen paper.

To plate Ladle the soup into bowls and top with a sprinkling of coriander, diced tomato and croûtons.

WINE SUGGESTION

I would choose an unwooded wine with lots of finesse, something like a good Chenin Blanc, as it tends to have a tropical fruit nose and a clean palate with good acidity, which would complement this soup well.

Cauliflower *and mushroom soup*

The cauliflower soup Melt the butter in a pan and gently sauté the cauliflower, onion, garlic, thyme and salt for 3–4 minutes. Do not let it brown. Add the stock and bring to the boil, then reduce the heat and simmer for 5 minutes. Pour the soup into a blender and blend until smooth. Stir in the coconut milk and add seasoning. Pass the soup through a fine sieve, then set aside and keep warm.

The mushroom soup Melt the butter in a pan and gently sauté the mushrooms, onion and garlic for 3–4 minutes. Do not let it brown. Add the mustard and cook for another minute. Add the stock and bring to the boil, then reduce the heat and simmer for 10 minutes. Pour the soup into a blender and blend until smooth. Stir in the cream, add seasoning and reheat.

To plate Place the soups in separate measuring jugs, then pour both soups at the same time into a warmed soup bowl, so that each soup fills half the bowl. Add a sprinkling of croûtons (see recipe, page 17), if desired.

This is a great duo – the cauliflower and mushrooms

seem to sing together. For a special occasion, add some

truffle oil just before serving.

CAULIFLOWER SOUP

20 ml butter

1 head cauliflower, broken
  into florets

100 g chopped onion

15 ml crushed garlic

10 ml fresh thyme

5 ml salt

500 ml vegetable stock
  (see recipe, page 153)

300 ml coconut milk

salt and freshly ground black
  pepper to taste

MUSHROOM SOUP

20 ml butter

250 g button mushrooms

250 g large field mushrooms

100 g chopped onion

7.5 ml crushed garlic

25 ml Dijon mustard

1 litre vegetable stock
  (see recipe, page 153)

200 ml double cream

salt and freshly ground black
  pepper to taste

SERVES 8

WINE SUGGESTION

I would choose a crisp, dry
Chardonnay.

Green asparagus *and truffle cream*

5 fresh spears green asparagus
per serving

50 ml black truffle juice
5 ml balsamic vinegar
200 ml grapeseed oil
20 ml white truffle oil
5 ml salt
a pinch of ground white pepper

wasabi paste

SERVES UP TO 12

The asparagus Prepare the asparagus by removing the leaves from three-quarters of the stem. Tie up in bundles of 10 with some string. Cook the asparagus in boiling salted water for 1 minute, then immediately refresh in ice water and remove the string.

The truffle cream Place the black truffle juice and balsamic vinegar in a blender. With the blender switched on to its fastest setting, gradually add the grapeseed and white truffle oils and blend until the dressing emulsifies. The cream should have a thick consistency. Add seasoning.

To plate Pour a little truffle cream into the centre of each serving plate. Arrange the asparagus spears as pictured alongside and dot wasabi around the edge of the truffle cream.

WINE SUGGESTION
Because of the richness of the truffle cream and the freshness of the asparagus, I recommend a wooded Sauvignon Blanc, as the gooseberry and asparagus flavours found in most Sauvignon Blancs will bring out the flavour of this dish.

I have Marco Pierre White to thank for teaching me how to make this when I was working with him. It is a stunning dish, simple yet full of flavour. The truffle cream is sufficient for 12 portions and will keep for one week in the refrigerator.

Greenhouse

the Greenhouse

Deep-fried goat's cheese, *French bean salad and mustard vinaigrette*

This dish is easy to make and delicious. It is ideal for dinner parties, as most of it can be made in advance and, as it is suitable for vegetarians, no one will miss out.

MUSTARD VINAIGRETTE

60 ml Dijon mustard
45 ml white wine vinegar
7.5 ml salt
2.5 ml whole white
    peppercorns
360 ml groundnut oil
45 ml hot water

GOAT'S CHEESE PARCELS

2 sheets springroll pastry
2 logs soft, plain goat's cheese
20 ml tapenade
oil for deep-frying

FRENCH BEAN SALAD

150 g French (green) beans
100 g skinned, seeded and
    coarsely chopped tomatoes
100 g diced onion

SERVES 8

WINE SUGGESTION

The best partner with goat's
cheese is Sauvignon Blanc
because of its crisp acidity
and fresh, fruity flavour.

The mustard vinaigrette In a bowl, combine the mustard, vinegar, salt and peppercorns. Using a hand blender, slowly blend in the oil to emulsify the vinaigrette. Add some hot water to thin it out. Refrigerate until ready to use.

The goat's cheese parcels Cut the pastry into quarters and do the same with the logs of cheese. Place a quarter of cheese on each quarter of pastry and top with half a teaspoon of tapenade. Wrap the pastry around the cheese so that it resembles the parcel pictured above and place in the refrigerator to firm up. Just before serving, deep-fry the parcels for 1 minute until golden brown.

The French bean salad Blanch the French beans in boiling salted water and refresh in ice water. Split the beans in half and add the diced tomato and onions. Add the mustard vinaigrette and toss to mix.

To plate Remove the beans, leaving behind the dressing and some of the tomato and onion, and place them in the centre of each plate. Top with a goat's cheese parcel. Spoon the tomatoes, onions and dressing around the plate.

Smoked salmon *with deep-fried oysters and four citrus beurre blanc*

This dish is a delightful combination of flavours and textures.

6 x 90 g portions smoked
    salmon
12 fresh oysters
100 g cake flour
2 eggs, lightly beaten
100 g dried breadcrumbs
vegetable oil for deep-frying
150 ml four citrus beurre blanc
    (see recipe, page 153)

GARNISH
fresh chervil or flat-leaf parsley

SERVES 6

The salmon Place a portion of smoked salmon in the centre of each plate.

The oysters Remove the oysters from their shells, making sure that you get rid of any grit. Roll the oysters in the flour, dip them into the egg and then the breadcrumbs to coat them. Make sure the oysters are evenly coated. Heat the oil until just before smoking hot, then deep-fry the oysters for 30 seconds.

To plate Place two oysters on each plate and garnish with chervil or flat-leaf parsley. Spoon the citrus beurre blanc around the plate.

WINE SUGGESTION
I find that Sauvignon Blanc
or a good Chenin Blanc
goes extremely well with the
smoked salmon, as it has
good, positive acidity.

Greenhouse

Sesame chicken salad *with honey and soy dressing*

The dressing Mix all the ingredients together and season with salt and pepper. Refrigerate until needed.

The chicken salad Cut the chicken breasts into thin strips, allowing 6–10 pieces per serving. Pour some of the dressing over the chicken pieces and set aside for a few hours in the refrigerator. Prepare a garden salad with your favourite salad leaves and herbs and set aside. Mix the flour and sesame seeds together and add salt and pepper. Remove the chicken from the dressing, pat dry and toss in the seasoned flour until evenly coated. Deep-fry the chicken pieces for a few minutes until golden brown. Drain excess oil on kitchen paper.

To plate While the chicken is still hot, arrange it on top of the prepared salad and serve immediately. Pour some dressing around the salad and garnish with fresh herbs.

Believe it or not, Liz McGrath found this recipe in a newspaper some years back. It was put on the menu and is now one of our signature lunch dishes.

6 chicken breasts, skinned and
    deboned
salad leaves and herbs to
    prepare a salad per person
85 g cake flour
100 g toasted sesame seeds
salt and freshly ground black
    pepper to taste
vegetable oil for deep-frying

HONEY AND SOY DRESSING
60 ml vegetable oil
60 ml extra virgin olive oil
30 ml sesame oil
30 ml soy sauce
30 ml honey
80 ml lemon juice
salt and freshly ground black
    pepper to taste

SERVES 6

WINE SUGGESTION
It is difficult to suggest a wine to go with this dish because of the dressing, but I would recommend an off-dry white like Riesling or Gewürztraminer with its exotic nose. This dish is also well suited to a light main course and, in this case, can be enjoyed with your favourite easy-drinking white wine.

Pan-fried Cape salmon, braised cucumber, roasted fennel, pommes aux crasse and basil cream

4 x 140 g portions Cape salmon

20 ml olive oil

12 baby fennel, roasted

salt and freshly ground black
  pepper to taste

BRAISED CUCUMBER

1 small English cucumber

100 ml water

50 g butter

POMMES AUX CRASSE

400 g new potatoes

20 g capers, rinsed and
  chopped

2.5 ml lemon zest

80 ml olive oil

5 ml salt

2.5 ml freshly ground
  black pepper

BASIL CREAM

100 g fresh basil leaves

1 baby onion, sliced

30 ml dry white wine

200 ml fresh cream

salt and freshly ground black
  pepper to taste

SERVES 4

WINE SUGGESTION

Try a fresh and zesty unwooded
Chardonnay, or perhaps even a
Viognier or Sémillon.

The salmon Pan-fry the salmon in the olive oil for 2 minutes per side.

The braised cucumber Peel and cut the cucumber lengthwise into three pieces, then cut each piece into four. Turn the cucumber into a barrel shape. Bring the water and butter to the boil in a pan, reduce the heat to a gentle simmer, then add the cucumber and cook for 4 minutes.

The pommes aux crasse Place the potatoes in a deep saucepan, cover with water and bring to the boil. Cook until soft, then remove and refresh. Peel the potatoes, then break them roughly with your fingers. Add the capers, lemon zest and olive oil and reheat. Add seasoning, then set aside until needed.

The basil cream Blanch the basil leaves for a few seconds, then refresh in cold water. Squeeze out any excess water and set aside. Place the onion and white wine in a pan and bring to the boil. Reduce the liquid by two-thirds, then add the cream, bring back to the boil and reduce slightly. Remove the pan from the heat. Place the basil leaves in a blender and pour the cream on top. Blend for a few minutes until the cream turns bright green in colour. Add seasoning and pass through a fine sieve. Set aside until needed.

To plate Pack 100 g pommes aux crasse in a large pastry ring cutter in the centre of each bowl, then carefully remove the ring. Arrange three pieces of cucumber and three fennel bulbs around the outside. Gently pour 50 ml basil cream around the pommes aux crasse. Place the salmon on top of the pommes aux crasse and serve.

Grilled yellowtail *niçoise*

Yellowtail is a very popular local fish and I find that it lends itself very well to this dish, which is quite full flavoured.

4 x 160 g portions yellowtail
20 ml olive oil
400 g new potatoes, cooked
   and peeled
100 g cherry tomatoes, halved
12 black olives, stoned and
   halved
100 g French (green) beans,
   blanched and split
2 baby onions, finely sliced
8 quail eggs, hard boiled
8 anchovy fillets

BALSAMIC DRESSING
50 ml balsamic vinegar
10 ml Dijon mustard
150 ml grapeseed oil
salt and freshly ground black
   pepper to taste

GARNISH
fresh chervil

SERVES 4

WINE SUGGESTION
Yellowtail is similar to tuna in
some ways and therefore needs
a fairly full-bodied wine to match
its gamey taste. My preference
is towards a wooded Sémillon
as it is not as buttery as
Chardonnay, but has lots
of fruit and freshness.

The balsamic dressing Place the balsamic vinegar and mustard in a blender and switch it on to a high setting. Slowly add the oil until the dressing emulsifies. Season and set aside.

The yellowtail Heat the oil in a pan and fry the yellowtail for 6–8 minutes. Set aside. Crush the new potatoes and mix with a little of the balsamic dressing.

To plate Place a large pastry ring cutter on each plate and pack in 100 g of potatoes. Arrange some tomatoes and an olive on top, then carefully remove the ring. Place the cooked yellowtail on top of the stack and garnish with French beans and onion slices. Cut the quail eggs in half and place them around the plate with the anchovy fillets and the rest of the dressing. Garnish with chervil and serve.

Prawns and avocado *with tomato salsa*

This is a very simple lunch dish that takes only minutes to prepare and serve. It also makes a great starter at a barbecue.

12 tiger prawns
2 avocados
salt and freshly ground black
    pepper to taste

1 onion, chopped
6 tomatoes, seeded and diced
1 red chilli, finely sliced
    (optional)
10 ml chopped fresh parsley
10 ml chopped fresh coriander
a pinch of salt
6 spring onions, finely sliced
5 ml lemon juice
30 ml olive oil

GARNISH
fresh chervil

SERVES 4

The prawns Cut down the back of the prawns, from head to tail, and remove the digestive tract with the point of the knife. Bring a saucepan of salted water to the boil and cook the prawns for 4 minutes. Remove and chill.

The tomato salsa Gently mix together all the ingredients and set aside in the refrigerator until needed.

To plate Cut the avocados in half, peel and seed, then place one half in the centre of each plate. Spoon the salsa around the plate and over the avocado. Arrange three prawns over the avocado, season, garnish and serve.

WINE SUGGESTION

Prawns have a delicate flavour so I would steer clear of any wine that is too heavy. A not-too-dry Sauvignon Blanc with an exotic nose, or an unwooded Chardonnay with good concentration, is recommended.

Roast fillet of beef

4 x 180 g fillets of beef

oil for frying

4 whole lamb kidneys, cleaned

24 baby button mushrooms

40 ml butter

40 ml water

4 large potato rosti
   (see recipe, page 160)

12 confit baby carrots
   (see recipe, page 161)

12 confit baby onions
   (see recipe, page 161)

160 ml red wine jus
   (see recipe, page 156)

WINE SUGGESTION

We mature all the beef used
in the restaurant ourselves,
and as a result the beef we serve
has a good, strong flavour.
To complement this dish
I would recommend a full-bodied
Cabernet Sauvignon, or blended
red with firm tannins and good
structure, as this brings out the
flavour of the beef beautifully.

The beef Pan-fry the fillets of beef in a little oil: 8 minutes for rare, 10 minutes for medium-rare, 12–14 minutes for medium, and 16–18 minutes for well done. Set aside. Pan-fry the kidneys in a little oil for about 1 minute. Set aside. Wash the button mushrooms and gently cook in the butter and water for 30 seconds.

The vegetables Reheat the potato rosti, and carrot and baby onion confits.

To plate Place one rosti in the centre of each plate and top with a piece of fillet. Place a kidney on top of the fillet, then arrange the carrots, baby onions and button mushrooms all around. Reheat the red wine jus, pour it over the beef and serve.

This is one of my signature dishes at the Cellars.

Every time I plate one I feel a great sense of delight

in its simplicity and beauty.

Hay-roasted rack of lamb

The pommes Anna Peel and slice the potatoes very thinly, then mix the slices with the butter and seasoning. Lightly grease four dariole moulds. Using 10 slices of potato per mould, line the inside of each mould, making sure the slices overlap. Pack the remaining potato slices in the moulds, taking care not to disturb the outside layer. Bake in a preheated oven at 180 °C until the potato is golden brown. When cooked, turn out of the mould and drain on kitchen paper.

The herb purée In a pan, gently sweat the shallot in the butter. Blanch the parsley in boiling water for 2–3 minutes, then drain. Add the spinach, watercress and parsley to the pan and cook for 5 minutes until soft. Drain excess water and chop to a coarse purée. Season. Return the purée to the pan, add the cream and bring the mixture to the boil, reducing it until thick. Set aside.

The butternut and parsnips Place the butternut discs and baby parsnips in an ovenproof dish and cook in the oven until soft. Set aside.

The lamb In a hot pan, seal the lamb until golden brown. Place a small amount of washed hay in an ovenproof roasting pan, then place the lamb on top. Roast in the oven at 180 °C (8–10 minutes for medium-rare, 10–12 minutes for medium).

To plate Reheat the pommes Anna in the oven at 180 °C for 2 minutes, then place it at the top of the plate. Place a disc of butternut in the centre of the plate and spoon some herb purée over it. Carve the rack of lamb and arrange it on top of the herb purée. Place the parsnips on the side. Drizzle over the red wine jus and serve.

I always use Karoo lamb as the meat is fantastic.
Lamb lends itself very well to hay-roasting,
bringing nature together in the oven.

4 discs chargrilled butternut
   (see method, page 34)
8 baby parsnips
4 x 4-bone racks of lamb
a handful washed hay
200 ml red wine jus
   (see recipe, page 156)

POMMES ANNA

4 large potatoes
100 ml clarified butter
   (see recipe, page 153)
salt and freshly ground black
   pepper to taste

HERB PURÉE

1 shallot, finely chopped
10 ml butter
a small handful fresh
   parsley sprigs
160 g spinach
a small handful watercress
salt and freshly ground black
   pepper to taste
40 ml double cream

SERVES 4

WINE SUGGESTION
Lamb is not a full-flavoured
meat and I would therefore
suggest a Merlot, with soft
tannins and good fruit.

Roasted butternut and Saint-Maure mille-feuille,
garden herb salad and sauce vierge

2 large butternuts
2 Saint-Maure goat's cheese
500 g fresh spinach
butter for frying
salt and freshly ground black
    pepper to taste
4 tomatoes, skinned, seeded
    and coarsely chopped
chopped fresh garden herbs

POTATO TUILE

1 large potato, peeled
100 g cake flour
2 egg whites
a small bunch chives, snipped

VIERGE BASE

300 ml extra virgin olive oil
100 ml lemon juice
10 coriander seeds

SERVES 4

WINE SUGGESTION

This is a lovely, light dish so
I would recommend a crisp,
dry Sauvignon Blanc with
good acidity.

The potato tuile Boil the potato until soft, then purée and leave to cool. Add the flour and egg whites and mix well to form a paste. Mix in the chives. On a non-stick baking sheet, spread the potato out with a palate knife to form 12 large discs. Place in a preheated oven at 100 °C and dry out the discs until they start to turn brown. Brush with olive oil, remove from the baking sheet and set aside.

The vierge base Mix all the ingredients together and set aside.

The butternut From the head of the butternut cut 8 x 1.5 cm-thick rings. Chargrill the butternut until brown grill marks appear (it also adds to the flavour) and then roast the butternut at 180 °C until just soft. Leave to cool, then cut with a pastry cutter into a perfect disc. Cut the goat's cheese into discs and arrange on top of the butternut. Place under the grill to melt. In a hot pan, sauté the spinach in a little butter until just wilted. Add seasoning. Warm the vierge base and add the tomatoes and fresh herbs.

To plate In the centre of each plate, build up layers using spinach, butternut and tuile. Spoon the vierge mixture around the plate and serve.

At the Cellars we always try our best to have innovative and original dishes on the menu for vegetarians. This dish was devised some time ago and the response has been very positive.

Strawberry *tart*

This dessert is perfect for summer and is an easy way of serving strawberries as unadulterated as possible.

4 sweet pastry tartlet cases
  (see recipe, page 161)

FILLING
200 ml crème pâtissière
  (see recipe, page 162)
200 g strawberries

DECORATION
80 ml strawberry coulis
  (see recipe, page 161)
icing sugar for dusting
fresh mint

SERVES 4

WINE SUGGESTION
The strawberries are not that
sweet and have good acidity,
so I would use this dish as the
perfect excuse to open a bottle
of Rosé 'Methode Cap Classique'
sparkling wine, preferably one
with a distinct berry nose.

The filling Spoon 50 ml crème pâtissière in each tartlet case and fill with whole, fresh strawberries.

To plate Place a tart on each plate. Decorate the plate with the strawberry coulis and dust the tarts with icing sugar. Top with fresh mint.

Passion fruit *soufflé*

No cookbook would be complete without a soufflé, an absolute classic. The passion fruit adds a lovely tang.

80 g butter, melted
100 g brown sugar
10 passion fruits (granadillas)
9 egg whites
a pinch of salt
150 g castor sugar
300 ml crème pâtissière
  (see recipe, page 162)

(see recipe, page 162)

DECORATION

passion fruit syrup
6 fresh strawberries
icing sugar for dusting
melted chocolate

SERVES 6

The soufflé Brush six soufflé moulds with melted butter, using upward strokes, and line with brown sugar. Cut the passion fruits in half and squeeze out the pulp. Pass the pulp through a fine sieve, then pour the liquid into a pan. Bring to the boil and reduce by half. Whisk the egg whites until soft peaks form. Add the salt and castor sugar and whisk again until firm peaks form. Mix the reduced passion fruit with the crème pâtissière, then mix in a quarter of the egg whites. When combined, gently fold in the remaining egg whites. Carefully spoon the mixture into the soufflé moulds and level the tops. Place in a preheated oven at 180 °C for 12 minutes until well risen.

To plate Wipe the ramekins clean as they come out of the oven and place on a plate. Serve immediately. If desired, make a syrup with the passion fruit pulp left over in the sieve: simply place the pulp in a heavy-based saucepan and add 250 ml water and 100 g castor sugar. Bring to the boil, stirring continuously. Simmer for 10 minutes, remove from the heat and chill until needed. Spoon this mixture onto the plate as decoration or serve as a side sauce that can be poured over the soufflés.

WINE SUGGESTION

Passion fruit is fairly acidic, so I would go with a Noble Late Harvest, as it would have a good concentration of residual sugar and enough acidity to match that of the passion fruit. If you can find a Noble Late Harvest with distinct passion fruit flavours, that is even better.

Chocolate plate *'Liz McGrath'*

250 g dark Callabaut or other
   good, dark Belgian chocolate
250 g unsalted butter
5 eggs
3 egg yolks
100 g castor sugar
250 g cake flour

250 ml milk
300 ml double cream
100 ml glucose
225 g castor sugar
225 g white chocolate
4 egg yolks

melted chocolate
icing sugar for dusting

The chocolate plate is a rich
and heavy dessert, so I
would recommend a sweet
red dessert wine.

The gâteau Melt the chocolate in a *bain-marie*. In a pan, melt the butter slowly and stir it into the chocolate. In a bowl, mix together the eggs, egg yolks and castor sugar until well incorporated. Add the warm, but not hot chocolate and butter mixture to the egg mixture, then fold in the flour. Spoon the mixture into eight buttered moulds and refrigerate for a few hours until chilled all the way through. Bake in a preheated oven at 200 °C for 10 minutes just before serving.

The ice cream Bring the milk, cream and glucose to the boil. Add half the sugar, stir well, then remove from the heat and stir in the white chocolate until melted. Mix together the remaining sugar and the egg yolks and incorporate it into the cream mixture. Strain. Churn in an ice-cream maker and freeze.

To plate Decorate a plate with melted chocolate then turn out the warm gâteau. Add a ball of white chocolate ice cream on the side. Dust with icing sugar.

A few years back, Jean-Christophe Novelli was hosted by the hotel during the Cape Gourmet Festival, and it was during this time that he made this dessert for Liz McGrath. She loved it, so he decided to name it after her. This dessert is a must for anyone who likes chocolate.

Floating *island*

This is a classic recipe for a classic dish.

MERINGUE

1 litre milk
6 egg whites
250 g castor sugar

CUSTARD

5 egg yolks
75 g sugar
1 litre milk
5 ml vanilla essence
200 ml Amarula liqueur

DECORATION

4 vanilla pods
flaked almonds, toasted
fresh mint

SERVES 4

The meringue In a saucepan, bring the milk to the boil, then reduce the heat so that the milk is just simmering. Whisk the egg whites with an electric mixer until soft peaks form, then add the castor sugar and whisk again until firm peaks form. Using two spoons, form four large quenelles from the meringue. Poach them in the simmering milk for two minutes, then turn them over and poach again. Remove from the heat and leave to cool.

The custard Mix together the egg yolks and sugar. Bring the milk to the boil and add the vanilla essence. Remove from the heat and slowly add the milk to the egg mixture. Mix in well, then return to a gentle heat, stirring, until the custard thickens slightly. Remove from the heat and stir in the Amarula. Set aside to cool.

To plate Float the meringue in a pool of custard. Decorate and serve cold.

WINE SUGGESTION

I would serve a sweet wine to match the sweetness in the meringue, but it should also have good acidity – something like a good quality White Muscadel.

The Cape Malay Restaurant is the brainchild of Liz McGrath who, in 1996, decided to showcase the Cape's unique cuisine to both local and international visitors.

Cape Malay cooking is unique to the Western Cape, and dates back to the 17th century, when ships trading spices from the East to Europe revittled in Cape Town. Their aromatic cargo was eagerly incorporated into the cuisine by the early settlers.

Chef Martha Williams is an expert in the authentic methods used in this style of cooking, and has compiled a menu featuring a selection of dishes, from the subtly smooth to the pungent and aromatic. Snoek soup, tomato bredie, bobotie, denningvleis and dhal curry star among a host of other imaginative dishes. The extensive wine list is specially designed to complement the gentle, spicy character of this cuisine.

Restaurant Manager Feroza Kazie and her friendly staff encourage guests to relax and eat in the true spirit of the Malay people – sharing with diners their knowledge of the food, life and culture of this colourful and vibrant community. In keeping with tradition, nothing is wasted, and all leftover food is given to the poor and needy.

The Cape Malay Restaurant

MARTHA WILLIAMS – **Head Chef**

Martha was born in a small village in the Langkloof mountains in the Western Cape, where she first learnt the skills of the kitchen from her mother, who was an excellent cook. Martha trained at a Chinese restaurant, where she was discovered by Liz McGrath, amd then spent five years in The Plettenberg kitchens, and subsequently, two years as Breakfast Chef at The Cellars-Hohenort in Constantia.

Before taking up her post as Head Chef at The Cape Malay Restaurant, Martha studied under Cass Abrahams, the foremost expert on Cape Malay culture and cuisine, who taught her the secret of the unique blends of herbs and spices used in this traditional cooking style.

Martha is regularly invited to present her culinary delights at national and international events, and recently demonstrated her Cape Malay cuisine skills at the Hotel Renaissance in Amsterdam.

Snoek *soup*

Snoek, one of the Cape's most popular fishes and widely available all along the coast, lends itself very well to Cape Malay cooking because of its flaky flesh and delicious flavour.

1 kg smoked snoek
1.5 litres water
25 ml butter
2 onions, finely chopped
salt and white pepper to taste
25 ml cornflour
mild curry powder to taste
250 ml full-cream milk

GARNISH
stiffly whipped egg white

SERVES 6–10

The soup Place the snoek and the water in a large saucepan and slowly bring to the boil. Reduce the heat and simmer for 1 hour or until the flesh falls off the bone. Strain the fish stock into another saucepan and set aside. Remove the fish from the bones, then discard the skin and bones. Add the fish to the reserved stock, bring to the boil and reduce by half. Set aside. Melt the butter in another saucepan and sauté the onions until golden. Add seasoning, cornflour, curry powder and milk, and cook until thickened. Add the fish and stock and cook for another 10 minutes.

To plate Ladle the hot soup into individual bowls and garnish with a spoonful of egg white just before serving.

WINE SUGGESTION
A full-flavoured white wine will complement this dish. Why not try a Viognier?

The Cape Malay Restaurant

Traditional Smoor Snoek

Smoor snoek is a traditional and very popular dish within the Cape Malay community. It is an imaginative way to use leftover snoek and an economical way to feed a lot of people. When I was a child, smoor *always meant the mixing together of lots of good things.*

750 g smoked snoek

125 ml sunflower oil

4 onions, sliced

5 medium potatoes, peeled
   and diced

10 ml crushed garlic

5 ml crushed fresh root ginger

5 whole cloves

3 whole allspice

2 red chillies, seeded and
   chopped

GARNISH

boiled, shredded green cabbage

freshly ground black pepper

crushed dried chillies

SERVES 6–8

The snoek Flake the fish, discarding any skin and bones as you go along. Set aside. Heat the oil and sauté the onions, potatoes, garlic, ginger, cloves and allspice, until the potatoes are almost cooked. Add the fish and chillies and continue to sauté until the potatoes are cooked. Do not remove the whole spices.

To plate Pack the snoek into a pastry ring cutter in the centre of each plate, then carefully remove the ring. Top with cabbage and sprinkle with black pepper and crushed chillies. Serve warm.

WINE SUGGESTION

Because the snoek has been smoked I would recommend a dry, fresh, crisp white wine, such as a Sauvignon Blanc, or a blended white wine.

The Cape Malay Restaurant

Fish bobotie

500 g hake steaks

10 ml chopped fresh parsley

6 fresh mint leaves, chopped

3 cloves garlic, crushed

10 ml soft margarine

a pinch of ground leaf masala

5 ml salt

a pinch of grated nutmeg

a pinch of freshly ground
    black pepper

1 small tomato, skinned and
    chopped

a pinch of turmeric

1 small onion, chopped

4 slices stale white bread,
    soaked in water for
    5 minutes

2 eggs, lightly beaten

SERVES 4

WINE SUGGESTION

Spicy food needs a spicy wine,
and a good example of this
is a Gewürztraminer, with its
characteristic exotic nose
of tropical fruit. An off-dry
Gewürztraminer works best.

The fish Place the hake in a steamer and steam the fish over medium heat for 10 minutes. Remove from the heat and allow to cool. Flake the fish and set aside.

The bobotie Mix together all the remaining ingredients, except the eggs, adding the bread last (do not squeeze all the water out of the bread or the mixture will be too stiff). Add the flaked fish to this mixture and spoon into an ovenproof dish or individual dishes. Bake in a preheated oven at 200 °C until lightly browned. Remove the dish from the oven and pour the beaten eggs over the fish mixture. Return to the oven for a further 10 minutes, or until it is browned on top.

To plate Serve individual portions with chutney (see recipe, page 155).

When you think of Cape Malay cooking, bobotie invariably springs to mind. Although it is traditionally made with minced meat, we have used fish as an interesting and unusual alternative.

Chicken livers *'peri-peri'*

The chicken livers Clean the livers, removing any tubes or membranes, and rinse. Mix together the chicken livers, flour, masala, salt and pepper. Toss in a hot pan with a little sunflower oil until almost cooked. Sauté the onions in a little oil in a separate pan until golden brown, then mix them in with the livers and continue to fry until the livers are cooked.

To plate Serve topped with parsley and crushed dry chillies to taste.

1 kg chicken livers, halved
280 g cake flour
15 ml masala
5 ml salt
5 ml freshly ground black
    pepper
sunflower oil for frying
2 medium onions, thinly sliced

GARNISH
chopped fresh parsley
crushed dried chillies

SERVES 8–10

I first cooked this dish at home for my children and, after tasting it, they kept asking me to prepare it for them again. I made a few changes here and there, refining the recipe a bit, and then decided that, seeing how much my children loved it, I would put it on the restaurant menu as well.

WINE SUGGESTION
It is almost impossible to find a wine to go with a peri-peri-style dish, but I would suggest a buttery Chardonnay if the dish is not too hot. As the heat increases, I would go with a sweet wine and, ultimately, with beer.

Bobotie

Bobotie is synonymous with Cape Malay cooking. It is a pungent, aromatic beef dish made with dried fruit and topped with baked custard. Bobotie can be traced as far back as the Middle Ages, when turmeric was brought from the East to Europe.

1 large onion, chopped

7.5 ml vegetable oil

25 ml butter

400 g beef mince

1 thick slice stale white bread

100 g sultanas

45 ml flaked almonds

20 ml chutney (see recipe,
   page 155)

1½ cloves garlic, crushed

7.5 ml masala

2.5 ml turmeric

5 ml ground cumin

5 ml ground coriander

2 whole cloves

2.5 ml peppercorns

2 whole allspice

5 ml dried mixed herbs

salt and freshly ground black
   pepper to taste

7 bay leaves

2 eggs, beaten

125 ml milk

SERVES 12

WINE SUGGESTION

My favourite wine with
this dish is a spicy
Shiraz and, failing that,
a fruity Pinotage.

The bobotie Fry the onion in the oil and butter until lightly coloured. Add the mince and fry gently for 2 minutes. Empty the mince into a colander and reserve the juice that drains from it. Soak the bread in the juice from the mince. In a mixing bowl, mix together the bread, mince, sultanas, almonds, chutney, garlic and all the spices and seasoning. Spoon the mixture into a large, ovenproof dish. Spike the bay leaves into the mixture. Combine the eggs and milk and pour it over the mince. Bake in a preheated oven at 200 °C for about 20 minutes until set.

To plate Serve with yellow rice and fruit chutney (see recipe, page 155).

Denningvleis

Denningvleis is a spicy meat dish flavoured with tamarind. The word denning *originated from the Javanese* dendeng, *meaning 'the meat of water buffalo'. Today, lamb or mutton is used to provide juiciness to an already flavourful dish.*

25 ml vegetable oil

3 large onions, sliced

5 cloves garlic, crushed

5 whole allspice

6 whole cloves

2 bay leaves

1 green chilli, finely chopped
(with seeds)

10 ml freshly ground black
pepper

375 ml boiling water

1 kg fatty mutton or lamb

25 ml tamarind

5 ml grated nutmeg

30 ml brown sugar

salt to taste

GARNISH

fresh parsley

SERVES 8–10

The meat Heat the oil in a large saucepan and fry the onions until they are transparent and soft. Add the garlic, allspice, cloves, bay leaves, chilli and pepper. Add 125 ml boiling water. Layer the meat on top of the onion mixture, cover the saucepan with a tight-fitting lid and leave to simmer for 30–40 minutes. Soak the tamarind in the remaining boiling water and allow to cool. Pour through a sieve, pressing all the juices through with a spoon. Pour the strained tamarind liquid over the meat and sprinkle with nutmeg and sugar. Season to taste and simmer for another 10–15 minutes.

To plate Garnish with parsley and serve hot with basmati rice and your choice of vegetables.

WINE SUGGESTION

I would recommend a light red wine with good fruit structure to go with this dish. Something like a Pinot Noir, or a light Merlot.

Tomato bredie

2 large onions, chopped
15 ml black peppercorns
820 g can whole, peeled
    tomatoes
25 ml sunflower oil
1 kg lean lamb, cubed
15 ml ground ginger
4 cardamom pods
5 ml whole cloves
410 g can tomato paste
2 medium potatoes, peeled
    and diced into 1 cm cubes
salt, freshly ground black
    pepper and brown sugar
    to taste

GARNISH
boiled potatoes, cubed
chopped fresh parsley

SERVES 6

The bredie Place the onions, peppercorns and tomatoes in a large casserole dish and bring to the boil. Keep boiling until all the liquid has cooked away. Add the oil and stir until the onions are golden brown. Add the lamb, ginger, cardamom pods and cloves and stir well. Reduce the heat, cover the dish with a lid and simmer for 3 minutes. Add the tomato paste and replace the lid. Leave to simmer for 20 minutes. Add the potatoes and seasoning. Replace the lid and simmer until the potatoes are cooked. Do not remove the whole spices.

To plate Garnish with the cubed potato and chopped fresh parsley, and serve with rice.

WINE SUGGESTION
Tomato is acidic so you will need a wine with a bit of residual sugar and soft tannins. Try a Cabernet Sauvignon/Merlot blend.

C Louis Leipoldt's description of bredies says it best: 'These are combinations of meat with vegetables so intimately stewed that the flesh is thoroughly impregnated with the vegetable flavour while the vegetables have benefited from the meat juices.'
(*Leipoldt's Cape Cookery*, W.J. Flesch & Partners, 1976)

Chicken biryani

The phyllo baskets Brush four sheets of phyllo pastry with melted butter and layer them one on top of the other. Cut these layered sheets into four equal squares, then place them over four large ramekins that have been sprayed with non-stick spray. Repeat with remaining phyllo pastry. Bake in a preheated oven at 150 °C until golden brown. Remove from the oven and set aside.

The biryani rice Boil the rice in salted water, with all the spices, until cooked. Strain and set aside.

The chicken Mix together all the ingredients, except the potatoes and seasoning, and leave to marinate for a few hours in the refrigerator. Remove the chicken from the marinade (do not wash or drain it) and fry very gently, being careful not to overcook it. Mix the chicken with the biryani rice and fried potatoes, and season well.

To plate Spoon the biryani into the phyllo baskets and garnish with hard-boiled eggs. If preferred, top with caramelized onions.

The royal chefs of Shah Jehan created biryani at the time of the Moghul Empire. They were the descendants of Genghis Khan, and seized power in India during the 16th century. They were known for their great taste, fine living and elaborate food, particularly the emperor's elegant meat and rice dishes (biryani).

PHYLLO BASKETS
8–12 sheets phyllo pastry
melted butter

BIRYANI RICE
400 g long-grain rice
4 bay leaves
15 ml masala
15 ml mother-in-law spice
15 ml turmeric
3 star anise

CHICKEN
500 ml Bulgarian yoghurt
10 ml mild curry powder
10 ml mixed spice
10 ml garam masala
5 ml turmeric
8 skinless, deboned free-range
    chicken breasts, cubed
2 medium potatoes, peeled,
    cut into small cubes and
    deep-fried
salt and freshly ground black
    pepper to taste

GARNISH
halved hard-boiled eggs

SERVES 8–10

WINE SUGGESTION
An off-dry or semi-sweet white wine will match the spicy rice and chicken.

The Cape Malay Restaurant

Chicken *pie*

These pies, with their delectable pastry, held centre stage as part of the Christmas celebrations in the 17th and 18th centuries. This recipe is an adaptation of what we usually serve in the restaurant. If preferred, the wine may be substituted with stock.

250 g ready-made flaky or
   puff pastry
2 hard-boiled eggs, sliced
beaten egg to glaze

FILLING

2 kg deboned chicken, cut
   into small pieces
6 allspice berries
6 peppercorns
3 whole cloves
2 medium onions, sliced
10 ml salt
200 ml chicken stock
   (see recipes, page 152)
300 g sago, soaked in water
   until soft
150 ml dry white wine
1 egg yolk mixed with a
   little milk
150 ml lemon juice

SERVES 8–10

WINE SUGGESTION

I usually serve this dish with
a light white wine with good
acidity, good fruit and a long
finish, like a Sauvignon Blanc
or Pinot Griggio.

The filling Stew the chicken pieces with the allspice berries, peppercorns, cloves, onions, salt and stock until tender. Add the sago to the chicken. Add the wine and simmer until the sago is transparent. Stir in the egg yolk mixture and lemon juice, then remove from the heat and set aside.

To assemble Roll out the pastry on a lightly floured surface to 5 mm thick and cut out pastry rounds to cover small pie dishes. Set aside. Spoon the cooled chicken filling into the pie dishes and place a few slices of hard-boiled egg on top. Cover with the reserved pastry rounds. Brush the pastry with a little beaten egg, then bake the pies in a preheated oven at 200 °C for 15–20 minutes.

To plate Serve hot with rice or on its own.

Chickpea and lentil *curry*

One of our regular guests asked me one day if I could make him a chickpea and lentil curry. I started playing around with the idea and this recipe was born. So here's to you Mr Levi.

400 g chickpeas

200 g brown lentils, soaked
   in water overnight

20 ml sunflower oil

2 medium onions, chopped

5 ml ground cumin

5 ml turmeric

15 ml roasted masala

5 ml crushed garlic

10 ml dried origanum

500 ml plain yoghurt

10 ml tomato paste

GARNISH

fresh coriander

SERVES 8 AS A MAIN
DISH AND 16–20 AS
A SIDE DISH

The curry Soak the chickpeas in hot water for 2 hours, then drain, cover with fresh water and bring to the boil. Cook until soft, then set aside. In a separate saucepan, bring the lentils to the boil in fresh water and cook until soft. Set aside. Heat the oil in a pan and brown the onions with all the spices and the garlic and origanum. In a bowl, mix together the yoghurt and the tomato paste, then add the onion mixture to it. Mix together the chickpeas, lentils and spiced yoghurt.

To plate Garnish and serve hot as a main dish or with a rice or fish dish.

WINE SUGGESTION

I have found that an off-dry Bukettraube works exceptionally well with this dish. The wine is aromatic and light, but has a good structure, and the sweetness matches the curry very well.

Dahl *curry*

2 medium onions, chopped

20 ml sunflower oil

15 ml whole cumin

1 stick cinnamon

4 cardamom pods

50 g each oil dhal, chana dhal
   and yellow mung dhal,
   mixed together and covered
   with water for at least
   30 minutes, or until swollen

410 g can tomato paste

7.5 ml turmeric

7.5–15 ml roasted masala
   (depending on how hot
   you like it)

15 ml ground cumin

15 ml ground coriander

4 cloves garlic, crushed

GARNISH

fresh coriander

SERVES 8–10

WINE SUGGESTION

I prefer a Riesling with
this dish, preferably an
off-dry one with pineapple
and mango tones.

The curry Sweat the onions in the oil and add the whole cumin. When the onions are cooked, add the cinnamon and cardamom pods. Cook for a few seconds over medium heat. Add the dahl and the water in which it was soaked, and bring to the boil. Add the tomato paste, then reduce the heat to low and simmer for about 15 minutes until cooked. Add the remaining ingredients and simmer for another 30 minutes.

To plate Garnish with coriander and serve hot with basmati rice.

Dhal has always been used in Cape Malay cooking
and is probably the most popular lentil dish.
Not only do lentils add flavour, but they are also
a great substitute for protein in a vegetarian diet.

Malva *pudding*

A delectably rich, warm, soft sponge pudding.

PUDDING

300 g sugar

4 eggs

180 ml apricot jam

120 g butter

500 ml milk

80 ml white vinegar

560 g cake flour

20 ml bicarbonate of soda

4 ml salt

SAUCE

1.125 litres fresh cream

500 g butter

600 g sugar

60 ml apricot jam

4 ml salt

SERVES 10

The pudding In a food processor, cream the sugar and eggs, then add the jam. Melt the butter and add it to the jam mixture. Add the milk and vinegar. Sift in the flour, bicarbonate of soda and salt, and mix. Pour the mixture into a 3 cm-deep baking sheet or pan and bake in a preheated oven at 180 °C for 40 minutes.

The sauce Place all the ingredients in a saucepan and bring to the boil. Let it boil for about 1 minute, then pour the hot sauce over the hot pudding.

To plate Serve with crème anglaise (see recipe, page 162).

WINE SUGGESTION

This dish is quite sweet and sticky, so I would recommend a sweet wine with good fruit and acidity, such as a good quality Hanepoot.

Milk *tart*

Milk tart (or melktert *as it is called in Afrikaans) dates as far back as the 17th century, when many Cape Malay cooks changed the basic Dutch custard pie by adding different flavourings, such as nutmeg and cinnamon.*

PASTRY

125 g butter

210 g castor sugar

5 ml vanilla essence

1 egg, beaten

140 g cake flour

140 g self-raising flour

10 ml sunflower oil

a pinch of salt

FILLING

1 litre milk

10 large eggs

250 g sugar

15 ml cake flour mixed to
    a paste with 30 ml water

2.5 ml ground cardamom

DECORATION

ground cinnamon

SERVES 10

WINE SUGGESTION

Milk tart is quite creamy and
not too rich, and I find that a
naturally sweet wine or Special
Late Harvest tends to go very
well with this dessert. The
important thing is that the wine
should not be too sweet.

The pastry Cream the butter and castor sugar, then add the vanilla essence. Add the egg, then gradually add the flours, oil and salt and work lightly to form a soft, pliable dough. Set aside in the refrigerator.

The filling In a saucepan, slowly bring the milk to the boil. Meanwhile, beat together the eggs and sugar. Remove the milk from the heat and pour it slowly into the egg and sugar mixture, stirring constantly. Continue stirring and add the flour paste. Set aside.

To assemble Lightly grease a heavy-based ovenproof dish with butter. Roll out the pastry on a floured surface, then line the dish with it. Pour in the filling and place small pieces of butter on top. Sprinkle with ground cardamom. Bake on the bottom shelf of a preheated oven at 200 °C for 40 minutes.

To plate Dust with cinnamon and enjoy as a dessert or as a cake with coffee.

The Cape Malay Restaurant

Koeksisters

The syrup Make this well ahead of time so that it can chill. In a large, heavy-based saucepan, dissolve the sugar in the water, stirring constantly. Bring to the boil, and boil for about 7 minutes, then remove from the heat. Add the golden syrup, cream of tartar, vanilla essence and lemon juice. Cool the syrup and refrigerate until needed.

The dough Sift together all the dry ingredients, then rub in butter until the mixture resembles fine crumbs. Add the milk and mix, then knead to a soft but pliable dough. Leave to rest for 15 minutes. Divide the dough into three equal-sized pieces and roll each out on a floured surface to about 5 mm thick.

To assemble small koeksisters Cut the dough into strips about 7–8 cm long by 1.5 cm wide. Take three strips and plait them. Press the ends together.

To assemble large koeksisters Cut the dough into strips about 12 cm long by 1.5 cm wide. Take three strips and plait them. Press the ends together.

To cook Keep the raw koeksisters covered with a damp cloth until needed. Heat the oil and deep-fry the koeksisters, a few at a time, until golden brown. Remove from the oil with a slotted spoon and submerge the koeksisters in the chilled syrup for about 30 seconds (it's a good idea to put the syrup bowl in ice while you work). Remove and place on a wire rack so excess syrup can drip off.

Some of my fondest childhood memories are of waking up early on Sunday mornings to the clatter of pots and pans and the smell of cinnamon and freshly made koeksisters. These delectable treats originate from Scandinavia, where koeksisters are a traditional dish.

SYRUP
2.8 kg sugar
1.75 litres water
15 ml golden syrup
7.5 ml cream of tartar dissolved
   in 15 ml cold water
20 ml vanilla essence
lemon juice to taste

DOUGH
560 g self-raising flour
2.5 ml salt
20 ml baking powder
125 g butter
500 ml milk
sunflower oil for deep-frying

MAKES ABOUT 18 LARGE,
36 SMALL KOEKSISTERS

WINE SUGGESTION
Koeksisters are traditionally
served with coffee or tea.

The Cape Malay Restaurant

Boeber

This dessert is based on the thick, spicy ceremonial drink, traditionally served hot on the 15th night of Ramadan to signify and celebrate the middle of the Fast.

125 g butter
250 g lokshen (vermicelli)
10 cardamom pods
3 sticks cinnamon
50 g sultanas
2 litres full-cream milk
75 g sago soaked in
   200 ml water for 30 minutes
100 ml sweetened
   condensed milk
15 ml rose water or
   10 ml vanilla essence
50 g blanched, flaked almonds
sugar to taste

DECORATION
flaked almonds, toasted

SERVES 10

WINE SUGGESTION
Boeber is a sweet pudding
so you will need a wine to
match it, but with good acidity.
Something like a good Jerepigo
or Muscadel.

The boeber Melt the butter in a deep saucepan, then add the lokshen and toss with a fork until lightly browned. Add the cardamom, cinnamon and sultanas, then pour in the milk and bring to the boil. Stir in the sago and the water in which it was soaked, and simmer for about 15 minutes until the sago is transparent. Stir constantly to prevent sticking. Mix in the condensed milk, rose water or vanilla essence, almonds and sugar and simmer for about 10 minutes until well blended.

To plate Serve hot in bowls, sprinkled with toasted flaked almonds.

The Cape Malay Restaurant

Sand
AT THE PLETTENBERG

This restaurant embraces views of Formosa Bay that are unsurpassed along this stretch of the beautiful South African coast. The mood is relaxed, the décor stylish contemporary, and the food modern South African.

Every five-star hotel must have an excellent à la carte restaurant, supported by a chef of note. The chef at the Sand, Christian Campbell, embraces the concept of using only the freshest fruits and vegetables from local farms, and fish straight from the sea.

CHRISTIAAN CAMPBELL – **Head Chef**

After training with top Michelin-star chefs in England, Christiaan worked in the kitchens of Raymond Blanc at Le Manoir aux Quat'Saison at Oxford, the legendary Roux Brothers at La Gavroche in London, at the elegant 16th-century Gravetye Manor, and at Chewton Glen, one of the most famous Relais & Chateaux country house hotels in Britain.

Christiaan returned to transform The Cellars restaurant from a table d'hote dining room to a Chaine des Rotisseurs-awarded restaurant. He also starred alongside Gary Rhodes when The Cellars-Hohenort hosted him on his visit to South Africa during the Cape Gourmet Festival.

After a sortie into the world of fromage, when Christiaan started The River Gate Cheesery in Franschhoek, he returned to The Collection as Head Chef at Sand.

Mussels in a Cape Malay broth

A lovely, vibrant broth with a combination of flavours that beautifully reflects all that is Cape Town. This broth can be enjoyed with all seafood. Some of the chicken stock can be substituted with the cooking juices from the mussels or with fish stock (see recipe, page 152) – the choice is yours.

The broth In a saucepan, sauté the onions in the 80 g butter until lightly coloured. Add the ginger and garlic, followed by all the spices. Sauté for a few minutes more. Add the chicken stock and boil rapidly for 15 minutes. Pour the broth into a blender and blend until smooth. Pass through a fine sieve, then return to the saucepan.

To plate Heat the mussels in the broth and, when they are hot, spoon the mussels into four wide soup bowls. Whisk the small cubes of butter into the remaining broth and season. Divide the broth between the four bowls and garnish with crisp sweet potato chips.

2 medium onions, chopped
80 g butter
2 cm piece fresh root ginger, grated
2 cloves garlic, crushed
30 ml masala
15 ml fennel seeds
15 ml ground coriander
15 ml turmeric
15 ml ground cumin
1 litre chicken stock
(see recipes, page 152)
48 mussels on the half shell, cooked
8 x 1 cm-cubes cold butter
salt and freshly ground black pepper to taste

GARNISH
sweet potato crisps

SERVES 4

WINE SUGGESTION
Villiera Rhine Riesling – 2001

Sand

Smoked salmon *wrapped in steamed butter lettuce*

160 g smoked salmon

16 large leaves butter lettuce

60 ml good quality mayonnaise

salt and freshly ground black
pepper to taste

12 baby potatoes, peeled and
cooked, then cut into 4 mm-
thick slices and marinated
in white wine vinaigrette
(see recipe, page 159)

2 baby fennel bulbs, cut into
strips and blanched in
boiling water until tender

10 ml caviar (optional)

CUCUMBER AND
LEMON PICKLE

20 ml white wine vinegar

30 ml peanut oil

30 ml olive oil blend

30 ml sugar

a pinch of salt

1 preserved lemon, flesh
discarded and the peel
finely diced

1 English cucumber, peeled,
seeded and cut into long,
thin strips

SERVES 4

WINE SUGGESTION

Danie de Wet –
Limestone Hill – 2002

The salmon Dice the salmon into 1 cm x 1 cm pieces and set aside.

The cucumber and lemon pickle With a whisk, combine all the ingredients, except the cucumber, in a mixing bowl. Toss the cucumber in the dressing and refrigerate until needed.

The lettuce Blanch the lettuce leaves in boiling water for a second and refresh in iced water. Drain the leaves on a kitchen towel. Using four leaves per portion, flatten them out on a clean work surface. Mix the salmon with 20 ml of the mayonnaise and add seasoning to taste. Divide the salmon into four equal portions and place it neatly in the centre of each portion of lettuce. Wrap up the salmon with the overlapping lettuce leaves. Place the salmon parcels in a steamer basket and steam for 4 minutes.

To plate Mix together the potatoes, fennel and remaining mayonnaise and season. Arrange the potato salad on four plates. When the salmon is just warm, remove from the steamer and place on top of the potato and fennel salad. Remove the lemon and cucumber pickle from the refrigerator and arrange some cucumber strips and caviar (if using) on top of the salmon. Spoon some of the pickle dressing onto each of the plates and serve immediately.

The smoked salmon is the focal point of this dish. The flavour of the salmon is elevated to new heights with the support of the fresh flavours of lemon, the crisp texture of cucumber, the creamy taste and texture of potato and mayonnaise, and the unique flavour of fennel bulb.
In addition to this, there is the contrast of the cold salad and the warm salmon, which makes this dish a tantalizing forerunner to whatever is to follow.

Seared prawns *in a lemon-paprika dressing on a cracked wheat salad with coriander pesto*

The lemon-paprika dressing Place all the ingredients in a blender and blend until smooth.

The cracked wheat salad Place all the ingredients in a bowl and toss to mix. Set aside until needed.

The prawns Pan-fry the prawns until just cooked. Spoon the dressing over the prawns and toss until well covered.

To plate Pack the cracked wheat salad into a pastry ring cutter in the centre of each serving plate, then carefully remove the ring. Arrange the prawns on top of the salad. Drizzle the coriander pesto around the edge of each plate and serve while the prawns are still hot.

This makes a lovely first course for a lunch on a hot summer's day. If you prefer, increase the number of prawns and serve as a main course.

20 medium prawns, cleaned
200 ml coriander pesto
  (see recipe, page 159)

LEMON-PAPRIKA DRESSING
125 ml chopped fresh coriander
125 ml chopped fresh parsley
1 clove garlic
20 ml paprika
20 ml ground cumin
a large pinch of saffron
140 ml olive oil
60 ml lemon juice
10 ml finely chopped sun-dried
  tomatoes

CRACKED WHEAT SALAD
60 ml fresh mint, chopped
125 ml snipped chives
8 spring onions, thinly sliced
500 ml tomato flesh, finely diced
300 ml fresh parsley, chopped
zest of 8 lemons
400 ml extra virgin olive oil
120 ml lemon juice
600 ml cooked bulgur wheat
salt and freshly ground black
  pepper to taste

SERVES 4

WINE SUGGESTION
Boschendal Sauvignon
Blanc – 2001

Mussel *and red pepper charlotte*

40 pieces steamed mussel meat

CRÊPES
110 g cake flour
1 egg
1 egg yolk
300 ml milk
a pinch each of salt and freshly
    ground black pepper
15 ml canola oil

ROASTED RED PEPPERS
4 large red peppers
40 ml extra virgin olive oil
salt and freshly ground black
    pepper to taste

RED PEPPER OIL
reserved ½ seeded, roasted
    red pepper
100 ml extra virgin olive oil
salt to taste

HERBED BUTTER
20 ml chopped fresh mixed
    herbs
60 g soft, unsalted butter
1 clove garlic, crushed
a pinch of salt

SERVES 6

WINE SUGGESTION
Waterford Sauvignon Blanc – 2001

The crêpes Sift the flour into a mixing bowl. Beat the egg and egg yolk and combine with the milk. Beat the milk mixture into the flour, then add the salt, pepper and finally the oil, beating constantly. Fry off six thin, small- to medium-sized pancakes. Set aside to cool.

The roasted red peppers Place the red peppers, oil and seasoning in a roasting pan and toss together. Roast at a high temperature until the skin of the peppers wrinkles. Remove from the oven and allow to cool until you are able to handle them. Carefully remove the skins and seeds. Set half of one pepper aside for the red pepper oil, then slice the remaining peppers into thin strips.

The red pepper oil Place the reserved half red pepper and oil in a blender and blend until smooth. Pass through a muslin cloth. Set in a conical strainer and and leave to slowly filter through. Add salt and set aside.

The herbed butter Mix all the ingredients together, then form the mixture into a small sausage shape. Place in the refrigerator until set.

To assemble Line six buttered moulds with the crêpes. Mix the peppers and mussel meat together, reserving a few mussels for the garnish. Fill each crêpe with this mixture. Cut six generous slices of the herbed butter and place one slice on top of each charlotte. Fold over the overlapping edges of the crêpes and wrap each mould with clingfilm. Place the mould in a steamer and steam the charlottes for 15 minutes.

To plate Gently turn out the charlottes onto serving plates. Heat the reserved mussel meat and place on top of the charlottes. Spoon over a little of the red pepper oil and serve at once.

The combination of these flavours was realized many years ago with a recipe Liz McGrath brought to me. I have modernized the form into what has become a delicious starter.

Sand

Warm chicken liver parfait *served with gorgonzola ravioli and a ruby port vinaigrette*

This full-flavoured starter is not as difficult to prepare as it may at first appear. Give it a try – it will be well worth it.

CHICKEN LIVER PARFAIT

1 small onion, chopped

10 ml butter

250 g fresh chicken livers, washed and trimmed

15 ml brandy

1 clove garlic, crushed

2.5 ml fresh thyme leaves

2.5 ml chopped fresh rosemary

2 eggs

1 egg yolk

140 g butter, melted

salt and freshly ground black pepper to taste

GORGONZOLA RAVIOLI

300 g cake flour

3 eggs

3 egg yolks

5 ml canola oil

salt to taste

6 x 20 ml softened gorgonzola

RUBY PORT VINAIGRETTE

750 ml port

1 onion, roughly chopped

2 cloves garlic, crushed

250 ml red wine

125 g sugar

1 bay leaf

100 ml balsamic vinegar

a sprig fresh thyme

2 white peppercorns

2.5 ml salt

75 ml extra virgin olive oil

salt and freshly ground black pepper to taste

SERVES 6

The chicken liver parfait In a pan, lightly sauté the onion in the 10 ml butter until just golden. Place the livers, sautéed onion, brandy, garlic, herbs, eggs and egg yolk in a blender. With the motor running, slowly add the hot, melted butter until it is all incorporated. Add seasoning. Pass the mixture through a sieve, then pour it into six well-oiled moulds to three-quarters full. Do not allow the mixture to cool before cooking. Arrange the moulds in a warm *bain-marie* and bake in a preheated oven at 100 °C for 30–35 minutes, or until just firm to the touch. Remove from the oven and leave to cool.

The gorgonzola ravioli Place the flour, 2 of the eggs, the egg yolks, oil and salt in a food processor and combine until a smooth dough forms. Do not overwork the dough. Using a pasta roller set on the thinnest setting, roll out a large sheet of dough. Beat the remaining egg, then lightly brush half the sheet with the egg. Arrange the gorgonzola in such a way that six round ravioli can be formed on the brushed part of the sheet. Fold the unbrushed section of pasta over the gorgonzola and press lightly around the cheese to expel any air bubbles. Using a pastry cutter, cut out the ravioli and set aside on a well-floured tray.

The ruby port vinaigrette Combine all the ingredients, except the oil and seasoning, in a pan. Bring to the boil and reduce to a quarter of the original volume. Pass through a fine sieve and set aside. Reserve the oil and seasoning until just before serving.

To plate Place the parfaits (in their moulds) back into a warm *bain-marie* and place in a moderate oven for about 10 minutes until warmed through. While the parfaits are in the oven, cook the ravioli in simmering water until the pasta is tender. Reheat the port vinaigrette and heat the reserved olive oil separately. Combine the two and season to taste. Turn out the parfaits onto serving plates and top each with a ravioli. Spoon over the port vinaigrette and serve at once.

Deboned quail *marinated in red wine and marmalade with a warm beetroot salad and orange dressing*

4 quails, portioned and deboned

QUAIL MARINADE

25 ml orange marmalade
75 ml red wine
5 ml crushed root ginger
1 clove garlic, crushed
a sprig each fresh thyme and
    rosemary
15 ml olive oil

BEETROOT SALAD

8 baby beetroot
20 ml olive oil
salt and freshly ground black
    pepper to taste

RED WINE VINAIGRETTE

25 ml red wine vinegar
25 ml olive oil
125 ml peanut oil
5 ml sugar
salt and freshly ground black
    pepper to taste

ORANGE DRESSING

300 ml orange juice
30 ml olive oil
30 ml peanut oil

SERVES 4

WINE SUGGESTION

Warwick Merlot or Verdun
Gamay Noir – 1999

The quail marinade Combine all the ingredients, pour over the quails and leave to marinate in the refrigerator for at least 24 hours.

The beetroot salad Toss the beetroot in the olive oil and add seasoning. Wrap the beetroot in aluminium foil and roast in a preheated oven at 180 °C until tender. Allow to cool, then peel the beetroot and cut into quarters.

The red wine vinaigrette Whisk together all the ingredients, then pour the dressing over the beetroot and leave to marinate overnight.

The orange dressing In a saucepan, bring the orange juice to the boil and reduce it to 90 ml. Remove from the heat. When cool, combine with the olive and peanut oils. Set aside.

The quails Remove the quails from the marinade and pan-fry them in a heavy-based, non-stick pan over medium heat until a lovely golden brown. Quickly turn the pieces over and cook for another minute.

To plate Reheat the beetroot in a saucepan, then arrange it on the serving plates. Place a quail on top of the beetroot and spoon over the roasting juices from the pan. Drizzle the orange dressing around the plate and serve at once.

Deboned quail dishes have always appealed to our guests, as they can be enjoyed without the fuss of having to fight with the bones. Beetroot is a greatly underrated vegetable, but I have found that it works particularly well with these little game birds. Their appeal is further enhanced by the flavours of citrus.

Roasted kingklip *with a crisp salmon and lemon grass risotto cake and cucumber spaghetti with wasabi dressing*

4 x 200 g portions kingklip
a little olive oil

RISOTTO CAKE

40 ml olive oil
1 small onion, finely chopped
10 ml grated fresh root ginger
1 clove garlic, crushed
200 g risotto rice
100 ml dry white wine
400 ml boiling chicken stock
   (see recipes, page 152)
salt and white pepper to taste
30 ml finely chopped fresh
   lemon grass
40 g smoked salmon, diced

CUCUMBER SPAGHETTI
WITH WASABI DRESSING

1 English cucumber, peeled,
   seeded and cut into thin,
   spaghetti-like strips
10 ml wasabi paste
10 ml rice wine vinegar
15 ml canola oil
2.5 ml salt

GARNISH

20 roasted asparagus spears

SERVES 4

WINE SUGGESTION

Steenberg Chardonnay –
unwooded – 2002

The risotto cake Heat the oil in a heavy-based pan and sauté the onion until tender. Add the ginger, garlic and risotto rice and sauté for 3 minutes. Slowly drizzle in the wine, followed by the chicken stock and seasoning, stirring all the time. Cook until the risotto is very thick and the rice is tender. Set aside to cool, then add the lemon grass. Once cool, take four medium-sized, round pastry cutters and fill halfway with the risotto. Divide the salmon among the four and then cover with the remaining risotto. Press down to make sure the risotto is packed firmly in the ring. Leave to cool completely before removing the ring.

The cucumber spaghetti with wasabi dressing Combine all the ingredients in a mixing bowl and set aside.

The kingklip Skin the kingklip portions. Heat the olive oil in a heavy-based pan and fry the kingklip until golden in colour. Transfer the fish to a baking sheet and roast at 200 °C for about 4 minutes.

To plate Dust the risotto cakes with flour and pan-fry until golden brown. Arrange a portion of cucumber spaghetti on each serving plate and set a portion of kingklip on top of the cucumber. Place a risotto cake on the plate and garnish with five roasted asparagus spears. Serve at once.

This one is a real showstopper, a wonderful collection of colour, contrasting flavours and textures, and is a must in the spring, when the new asparagus comes into season. The supporting cast – the cucumber, wasabi and salmon – provide a wonderful setting for the roasted kingklip.

Sand

Grilled sole with creamed leeks and mashed potato
and tempura calamari scented with lemon

The leek purée Melt the butter in a saucepan and sweat the onion, leeks and thyme until the onion and leeks are soft. Add the wine and reduce until syrupy. Add the cream and bring to the boil. Remove from the heat, pour into a blender and blend until smooth. Set aside.

The mashed potatoes Boil the potatoes in their jackets until tender. Peel and mash them, gradually beating in the milk until smooth and creamy. Set aside.

The tempura Infuse the water with the zest and allow to cool. Pass through a sieve and refrigerate until well chilled. Place the batter mix into a small mixing bowl and slowly stir in the infused water until a smooth batter forms.

The soles Season the soles, then brush with olive oil and pan-fry until golden. Remove from the pan and place on a baking sheet, then finish off under the grill. The soles are cooked when the flesh lifts easily from the bone.

The calamari Dust the calamari rings in the flour, season with salt and dip into the tempura batter. Deep-fry in hot oil until golden in colour.

To plate Reheat the mashed potatoes and leek purée, then combine them and beat in the butter and seasoning. Form the creamed leeks and potatoes into a cake on each serving plate and garnish with a little spinach or rocket. Arrange the calamari on top of this. Remove the soles from the grill and plate.

Grilled soles are delicious on their own. However, with the addition of deliciously flavoured mashed potatoes, the experience can be prolonged. In this recipe, calamari in batter makes a dramatic comeback.

4 dressed West Coast soles
salt and freshly ground black
    pepper to taste
olive oil for brushing
16 calamari rings
cake flour for coating
canola oil for deep-frying

LEEK PURÉE
20 ml butter
1 small onion, finely chopped
2 leeks, finely chopped
2.5 ml fresh thyme
125 ml dry white wine
100 ml fresh cream

MASHED POTATOES
3 medium potatoes
100 ml hot milk
50 g butter, cubed
salt and freshly ground black
    pepper to taste

TEMPURA
300 ml hot water
zest of 3 lemons
125 ml tempura batter mix

GARNISH
spinach or rocket

SERVES 4

WINE SUGGESTION
Iona Sauvignon Blanc – 2002

Grilled pork cutlets *with bean and corn ragout, and sage and apple compote*

8 pork cutlets

SAGE AND APPLE COMPOTE

1 medium onion, chopped

30 ml canola oil

15 ml grated fresh root ginger

5 ml yellow mustard seeds

400 ml verjuice

150 g chopped dried apple

15 ml finely chopped fresh sage

BEAN AND CORN RAGOUT

100 g white beans, soaked in
    water overnight

300 ml chicken stock
    (see recipes, page 152)

1 small stick celery

1 small onion, chopped

1 leek, chopped

1 carrot, peeled and chopped

1 clove garlic, crushed

40 ml butter

100 ml dry white wine

400 ml fresh cream

4 whole corn on the cob,
    cooked and shucked

2.5 ml fresh thyme

2.5 ml finely chopped fresh
    rosemary

SERVES 4

WINE SUGGESTION

Hamilton Russell
Chardonnay – 2001

The sage and apple compote Sauté the onion in the oil until lightly coloured, then add the ginger and mustard seeds, followed by the verjuice. Add the dried apple and simmer gently until the apple is tender. If the compote starts to cook dry, add a little more verjuice. Once the apple compote is cooked, set aside to cool, then add the sage.

The bean and corn ragout Drain the beans and place them in a saucepan with the chicken stock. Simmer until the beans are tender. Remove from the heat and leave the beans to cool in the cooking liquid. In a separate pan, sweat the vegetables and garlic in the butter until tender. Add the white wine and reduce. Add the chicken stock (drained from the beans) and reduce until less than 100 ml remains. Remove from the heat, stir in the cream and reduce by half. Remove from the heat and strain into a clean saucepan, squeezing out all the sauce. Add a quarter of the cooked beans to this sauce and simmer for 5 minutes. Pour into a blender and blend until smooth. Pass through a fine sieve, then combine with the remaining beans, the corn and the herbs.

The pork cutlets Season the cutlets well, then grill them on an open-flame kettle barbecue until just cooked.

To plate Reheat the ragout and season well. Dish up a spoonful of ragout on each serving plate. Arrange the grilled cutlets and the sage and apple compote on the plates and serve.

The recipe for this dish is very simple. Always take great care with simple recipes, for the outcome and flavour of the dish will very much depend on the skill and care that you place into the cooking thereof, as there are not a lot of strong flavours and spices to mask any shortcomings.

Sand

Rack of Karoo lamb, *with ratatouille and crushed potatoes flavoured with chevin*

2 whole lamb racks, trimmed
　　and chine removed
salt and freshly ground black
　　pepper to taste
30 ml extra virgin olive oil
2 medium potatoes, cooked,
　　peeled and roughly diced
100 g fresh white goat's cheese
5 ml each chopped fresh
　　rosemary and thyme
20 ml basil pesto (see recipe,
　　page 159)

RATATOUILLE
1 small aubergine (brinjal)
1 small onion
1 red pepper
1 yellow pepper
2 courgettes (baby marrows)
olive oil for frying

TOMATO SAUCE
410 g can whole Italian tomatoes
15 ml balsamic vinegar
10 ml sugar
salt and freshly ground black
　　pepper to taste
500 ml extra virgin olive oil
a sprig fresh thyme

SERVES 4

WINE SUGGESTION
Oude Weltevreden
Chardonnay – 2000

The ratatouille Dice the vegetables into equal-sized pieces, then sauté each vegetable separately in the olive oil until tender. When finished with each vegetable, immediately transfer it to an ice *bain-marie* to retain its colour.

The tomato sauce Place all the ingredients, except the olive oil and thyme, in a heavy-based saucepan and simmer for 15 minutes. Heat the oil separately, then add it to the tomato mixture. Add thyme to taste. Pour the mixture into a blender and blend until smooth, then pass through a sieve. Set aside.

The lamb Season the lamb and seal in a hot pan in olive oil until evenly browned. Transfer to the oven and roast at 200 °C for about 10 minutes. Remove from the oven and leave to rest in a warm place for 6 minutes.

The potatoes Reheat the potatoes and add the crumbled goat's cheese and herbs. Season to taste.

To plate In a saucepan, combine the ratatouille vegetables with some of the tomato sauce and heat through. Spoon the potatoes and the ratatouille onto the serving plates. Carve the racks of lamb and share out the portions. Garnish the ratatouille with a spoonful of basil pesto.

The crushed potatoes accompanying this dish are very morish. The goat's cheese can be substituted with cow's milk pecorino, which is equally delicious.

Sand

Oven-roasted springbok loin *with onion, sultana and garlic compote*

The onion, sultana and garlic compote Melt the butter in a pan and sauté the garlic over a gentle heat until a beautiful golden colour. Add the sultanas, wine, sugar and thyme and reduce until the sauce develops a light syrup consistency. Strain the sauce, reserving the sultanas and garlic, and return the juice to the pan. In a separate pan, sauté the baby onions in a little olive oil until golden. Transfer the onions to the pan with the strained, reduced sauce and gently cook in the sauce until the onions are tender. Return the sultanas and garlic to the pan, then remove from the heat and set aside.

The caramelized sweet potato Wrap each potato separately in aluminium foil and bake at 180 °C until just tender. Remove the foil and leave to cool. Peel and cut the potatoes into rough cubes. Melt the butter in a heavy-based, non-stick pan and sauté the potatoes over a moderate heat until they caramelize. Season.

The springbok Season the springbok well and pan-fry in a little butter until evenly browned. Transfer to a roasting pan and roast at 200 °C for about 5 minutes. Remove from the oven and leave to rest for 5 minutes before carving.

To plate Place the caramelized sweet potato in the centre of each plate. Cut each loin in half, at a slant, and place on top of the sweet potato. Spoon the compote around the edge of the plate and garnish the loin with sweet potato crisps.

Our foreign diners love this dish. The caramelized sweet potatoes deliver a wonderful sticky vanilla flavour, which, together with the sun-ripened flavour of sultanas, provides an ever-so-slight sweetness that works very well with the springbok loin.

4 x 200 g portions springbok loin
salt and freshly ground black pepper to taste
80 g butter

ONION, SULTANA AND GARLIC COMPOTE
80 g butter
60 ml halved cloves garlic, blanched in boiling water
115 g sultanas
750 ml semi-sweet white wine
30 ml sugar
a sprig fresh thyme
20 baby onions, peeled
olive oil for frying

CARAMELIZED SWEET POTATO
2 large sweet potatoes
100 g butter
salt and freshly ground black pepper to taste

GARNISH
sweet potato crisps

SERVES 4

WINE SUGGESTION
Saxenburg (Private Collection) Pinotage – 1996

Sand

Grilled chicken breast *with batons of polenta chips and truffle-scented jus*

4 large, plump chicken breasts

olive oil for rubbing

salt and freshly ground black
   pepper to taste

250 ml roast chicken jus
   (see recipe, page 156)

8 small cubes butter

5 ml truffle oil

12 roasted asparagus spears

4 courgettes (baby marrows),
   sliced lengthwise and sautéed

POLENTA BATONS

375 ml fresh cream

375 ml chicken stock
   (see recipes, page 152)

170 g quick-cooking polenta

30 ml grated Parmesan

a bunch spring onions, finely
   sliced at an angle

¼ red chilli, seeded and
   finely chopped

salt and freshly ground black
   pepper to taste

olive oil for frying

SERVES 4

The chicken Rub the chicken breasts with olive oil and seasoning and arrange in a roasting pan. Place under the grill. Turn regularly until the chicken is beautifully browned and crispy. Set aside and keep warm.

The polenta batons In a heavy-based saucepan, bring the cream and chicken stock to the boil. Whisk in the polenta and let it cook for 3 minutes. Remove from the heat and stir in the Parmesan, spring onions and chilli. Add seasoning. Spoon the polenta onto a small baking sheet lined with silicone paper and smooth it out to a depth of 1 cm. Leave to cool, then cut into strips 1 cm wide and 6 cm long. Heat a non-stick frying pan and fry the polenta batons in hot oil until golden and crispy. Remove with a slotted spoon and place on kitchen paper to drain excess oil.

To plate In a saucepan, bring the chicken jus to the boil and whisk in the butter. When the butter is incorporated, remove from the heat and whisk in the truffle oil. Arrange the polenta batons and chicken breasts on the serving plates. Spoon over liberal quantities of the sauce and serve at once.

WINE SUGGESTION

Hamilton Russell

Chardonnay – 2001

The flavour of the chicken is enhanced by the addition of the aromatic truffle-scented jus.

Passion fruit *chiboust*

CRÈME PÂTISSIÈRE

220 ml passion fruit
    (granadilla) juice
70 ml orange juice
250 ml fresh cream
7 egg yolks
100 g sugar
40 g cake flour
4 sheets gelatine

MERINGUE

100 ml water
225 g sugar
7 egg whites

DECORATION

icing sugar for dusting

SERVES 10

The crème pâtissière Place the passion fruit juice, orange juice, cream, egg yolks and sugar in a saucepan and whisk over a moderate heat. When the mixture starts to thicken, remove from the heat and gradually whisk in the flour. Return to the heat and stir until the mixture thickens completely. Spoon 30 ml of the mixture into a pan and heat gently over a low heat. Cover the gelatine sheets with a little cold water for 5 minutes, then squeeze out the excess liquid. Add the gelatine to the pan and stir over a medium heat, then add it to the passion fruit mixture, mixing well. Set aside to cool.

The meringue In a saucepan, bring the water and sugar to the boil, and boil for about 5 minutes. Meanwhile, whisk the egg whites in a food processor until stiff peaks form. While the machine is still running, pour the syrup into the egg whites and whisk for another 7–8 minutes. Fold the meringue into the passion fruit mixture, adding a few passion fruit pips to enhance the appearance. Pour the mixture into individual moulds or, for creative flair, into passion fruit half-shells. Place in the refrigerator to set.

To plate When set, remove the passion fruit chibousts from the refrigerator and dust with icing sugar. Arrange them on a baking sheet and place under a hot grill to caramelize the tops. Serve on dessert plates.

WINE SUGGESTION

Neethlingshof Weisser Riesling
Noble Late Harvest – 1998

Brought to us by Christophe, a visiting chef from Paris, this delicate, light dessert is a lovely way to end a good meal.

Sand

Date pudding *with rum-and-raisin ice cream and sweet potato spaghetti*

A lovely spin on a great traditional dessert. The ice cream and sweet potato work like a charm with this baked pudding.

125 ml crème anglaise (see recipe, page 162)

PUDDING

250 g dates
250 ml hot water
5 ml bicarbonate of soda
125 g butter at room temperature
200 g brown sugar
2 eggs
240 g cake flour
5 ml baking powder
2.5 ml salt
5 ml ground cinnamon
5 ml ground ginger
a pinch of grated nutmeg
100 g pecan nuts, chopped

SYRUP

200 g brown sugar
15 ml butter
185 ml water
1 stick cinnamon
10 ml vanilla essence
a pinch of salt
125 ml dark rum

RUM-AND-RAISIN ICE CREAM

115 g raisins
125 ml dark rum
750 ml fresh cream
350 g castor sugar
800 ml milk
200 g glucose
18 egg yolks

SWEET POTATO SPAGHETTI

2 sweet potatoes
750 ml sunflower oil for deep-frying
50 g ground cinnamon
50 g icing sugar

DECORATION

icing sugar for dusting

SERVES 6

The pudding Line a 24 cm diameter tart tin, or 6 individual 10 cm diameter tins with silicone paper. In a saucepan, bring the dates and water to the boil. Add the bicarbonate of soda, then remove from the heat and leave to cool. Beat the butter until fluffy, then add the sugar. After all the sugar is incorporated, beat in the eggs one at a time. Sift the flour, baking powder, salt, cinnamon, ginger and nutmeg and add to the butter mixture. Stir in the nuts, then pour the mixture into the tin and bake in a preheated oven at 180 °C until golden brown (about 40 minutes for a large tin, and about 15 minutes for individual tins).

The syrup Mix together the sugar, butter and water in a saucepan and simmer over a low heat. Cook for about 1 minute, then add the cinnamon. Remove from the heat and stir in the remaining ingredients. Pour the warm syrup over the hot pudding.

The rum-and-raisin ice cream Soak the raisins in the rum to soften them. In a saucepan, bring the cream, castor sugar, milk and glucose to the boil. In the meantime, beat the egg yolks until light and foamy. Add the beaten egg yolks to the hot cream mixture, and stir until thick. Ensure the mixture does not boil after the eggs have been added as this will cause the mixture to separate. Add the soaked raisins, then leave the mixture to cool to room temperature. Churn in an ice-cream maker and freeze for about 4 hours until the ice cream is set.

The sweet potato spaghetti Use a mandolin to slice the sweet potatoes, then cut the slices into spaghetti-like strips. Place the strips in a small sieve to form a bundle, then deep-fry until golden. Combine the cinnamon and icing sugar and dust over the spaghetti bundle while it is still warm.

To plate Pour the crème anglaise into a dessert bowl and place a portion of pudding in the centre and dust with icing sugar. Place a scoop of ice cream on top of the pudding, then finish it off with sweet potato spaghetti.

WINE SUGGESTION

Klein Constantia Vin de
Constance – 1997

Sand

Chocolate tart *with chocolate sorbet*

PÂTÉ SUCRÉE

250 g soft butter

250 g castor sugar

2 eggs

500 g flour

50 g finely ground almonds

CHOCOLATE FONDANT

250 ml fresh cream

600 g dark Callebaut Belgian
  chocolate, cut into small
  pieces

3 eggs

4 egg yolks

70 g butter

CHOCOLATE SORBET

500 ml water

200 g sugar

300 g bitter chocolate, cut into
  small pieces

10 ml brandy

60 g cocoa powder

GARNISH

cocoa powder for dusting

SERVES 10

WINE SUGGESTION

Steenberg Brut Methode Cap
Classique – Non-vintage

The pâté sucrée Place all the ingredients in a blender and blend until they form a pliable dough. Wrap up tightly in clingfilm and place in the refrigerator for at least 1 hour to rest. Roll out the dough on a lightly floured surface to 5 mm thick, then line ten 10 cm-diameter individual tartlet tins (or a 25-cm diameter tart tin). Bake in a preheated oven at 180 °C until golden brown (15 minutes for individual tartlet tins, and about 25–30 minutes for a large tart tin).

The chocolate fondant In a heavy-based saucepan, bring the cream to the boil, then remove from the heat. Stir in the chocolate, eggs and the egg yolks until combined. Slowly whisk the butter into the chocolate mixture until it reaches truffle consistency. Set aside.

The chocolate sorbet Combine the water and sugar and bring the mixture to the boil. Allow to boil for 3 minutes. Remove the sugar mixture from the heat and whisk in the chocolate, brandy and cocoa. Pour the mixture through a sieve and leave to cool. Place the mixture in an ice-cream maker and churn to form a soft, scooping consistency.

To plate Place a 60 ml scoop of chocolate fondant into each tartlet or all the fondant into the large tart and bake for approximately 8 minutes at 120 °C. Remove from the oven and place in the refrigerator to cool and set. When the tartlet has cooled, carefully remove it from the mould onto a dessert plate and serve with a scoop of chocolate sorbet. Dust with cocoa powder.

This dessert needs no explanation or introduction. It is a must for anyone who loves to indulge in the magic of chocolate.

Sand

Chocolate marquise *with a raspberry sabayon and hazelnut biscuits*

The chocolate marquise Whisk together the egg yolks and sugar, then whisk in the melted chocolate. In a separate bowl, whisk together the butter and cocoa, then add it to the chocolate-egg mixture. Fold in the whipped cream. Spoon the mixture into six individual moulds and freeze for up to 2 hours.

The raspberry sabayon Whisk the egg and egg yolks over a double boiler until light in colour and fluffy. Add the raspberry purée to the egg mixture. In a saucepan, bring the wine and liqueur to the boil, then remove from the heat and gradually add it to the egg mixture, whisking continuously until the sabayon is light and foamy.

The hazelnut biscuits Mix together the hazelnuts, castor sugar and flour. In a separate bowl, beat the egg whites until foamy, then add the butter. Stir the hazelnut mixture into the butter mixture – it should resemble a paste. Line a baking sheet with silicone paper. Take a sheet of clean, hard plastic or stiff board (large enough to fill the baking sheet) and cut out decorative shapes. Lay the sheet or board template on top of the silicone paper and spread the biscuit paste over the top. Carefully lift the plastic or board, leaving the decorative biscuit shapes behind. Bake in a preheated oven at 180 °C for about 8 minutes.

To plate Turn out the marquises onto serving plates and leave to stand for at least 20 minutes at room temperature before serving. Spoon the sabayon onto the plates and garnish the marquises with the hazelnut biscuits.

This rich chocolate mousse is refreshed with a variation on the classic sabayon.

CHOCOLATE MARQUISE
6 egg yolks
200 g sugar
145 g dark Callebaut Belgian
    chocolate, melted
250 g soft butter
165 g cocoa powder
500 ml fresh cream, whipped

RASPBERRY SABAYON
1 egg
5 egg yolks
250 ml raspberry purée
250 ml sweet white wine
    (Noble Late Harvest)
50 ml Kirsch liqueur

HAZELNUT BISCUITS
150 g ground hazelnuts
270 g castor sugar
60 g cake flour
5 egg whites
100 g butter, melted

SERVES 6

WINE SUGGESTION
Rust en Vrede Cabernet
Sauvignon – 1999

A *trio of* fruit jellies with crème anglaise

This is a complete remake of the old boarding school classic – jelly and custard. This time round, however, we have added passion and finesse to make this old favourite last well into the next century.

CRÈME ANGLAISE
3 egg yolks
30 ml castor sugar
250 ml milk
½ vanilla pod

RASPBERRY JELLY
500 ml water
500 g sugar
250 g raspberries
5 leaves gelatine

PASSION FRUIT
(GRANADILLA) JELLY
500 ml water
500 g sugar
125 ml passion fruit pulp
6 leaves gelatine

MANGO JELLY
500 ml water
500 g sugar
pulped flesh of 3 mangoes
5 leaves gelatine

SERVES 10

WINE SUGGESTION
Neethlingshof Weisser Riesling
Noble Late Harvest – 2000

The crème anglaise In a bowl, beat together the egg yolks and castor sugar. In a saucepan, bring the milk and vanilla pod to the boil. Discard the vanilla pod and pour the hot milk into the egg-sugar mixture, stirring well. Pour this mixture into a clean saucepan, return to the heat and cook over a low heat until the mixture achieves a pouring consistency. Pass through a fine sieve.

The fruit jellies For each jelly, bring the water, sugar and fruit pulp to the boil, then remove from the heat and set aside to cool. Sponge the gelatine leaves in a little cold water, then heat to dissolve the gelatine. Add the gelatine to the fruit syrup, making sure that no lumps form. Pour the mixture into 50 ml moulds and leave in the refrigerator until set.

To plate Place one of each jelly on a plate and pour over the crème anglaise.

P A V I L I O N

AT THE MARINE

Pavilion is the perfect example of the modern restaurant of today: relaxed and informal, but with an understated elegance. The décor is fresh and sophisticated, using rich cream and other natural shades to enhance the restaurant's ambience.

The view of the sea is exceptional and adds another dimension to the dining experience. During the months of June to December, when the southern right whales visit Walker Bay, diners can also experience the world's best land-based whale-watching from their table.

LOUIS VAN REENEN – **Head Chef**

Louis van Reenen is one of a new breed of South African chef – well travelled, and with a passion for food. Inspired by British chefs, it is no surprise that Louis classes his food as contemporary South African with a British influence.

Louis spent a year on a kibbutz before attending the Swiss Hotel School in Mmbatho, where he met his mentor and source of inspiration, Michel Gehrig, a brilliant Swiss chef. Louis trained in some of South Africa's top kitchens, including Zimbali Lodge, but it was at the Cardiff Hilton in Wales that he 'graduated from being a cook to a chef'. Since then, he has worked at many Michelin-star restaurants under some of the greatest chefs in the world.

At The Marine, he oversees both the Pavilion and Seafood restaurants, where his aim is to give his guests an unforgettable gastronomic experience.

Roast tomato and ratatouille soup *with basil foam*

The roast tomato soup Sprinkle the salt and thyme in a roasting pan. Place the tomatoes, flesh side down, on top of the salt and thyme. Roast in a preheated oven at 180 °C for about 20 minutes until the skin starts to crisp. Sweat the onions in a saucepan, then add the roast tomatoes. Simmer over a low heat for 45 minutes. Place in a blender and blend until smooth. Set aside.

The ratatouille Cut the peppers, courgette, aubergine and tomato into small cubes and sauté in the oil until just tender. Add seasoning. Add the basil pesto just before serving.

The basil foam Bring the milk to the boil, then add the fresh basil. Season with salt. Pour into a blender and blend until very foamy.

To plate Heat the tomato shells in the oven, then spoon the ratatouille vegetables into them. Place a tomato in the centre of each warm soup plate and pour the soup around the tomato. Spoon the basil foam around the tomato and serve.

Note: This soup is suitable for vegetarians. In the case of vegans or those with lactose intolerance, omit the Parmesan from the pesto and leave out the foam altogether.

The intense flavour of South African tomatoes creates an exceptional soup. And nothing complements tomato as well as fresh basil.

6 plum tomatoes, skinned and
   seeded to leave a shell

ROAST TOMATO SOUP
75 ml rock salt
a large handful fresh thyme
30 plum tomatoes, halved
6 medium onions, peeled and
   roughly chopped

RATATOUILLE
¼ green pepper
¼ red pepper
¼ yellow pepper
¼ large courgette (baby marrow)
⅛ aubergine (brinjal)
1 plum tomato, skinned
   and seeded
30 ml olive oil
salt and freshly ground black
   pepper to taste
15 ml basil pesto (see recipe,
   page 159)

BASIL FOAM
300 ml low-fat milk
a large handful fresh
   basil leaves
salt to taste

SERVES 6

WINE SUGGESTION
Môreson Chenin Blanc – 2000

Fresh Knysna oysters *with a chilli and lime sorbet*

Some of the best oysters are found along our coastline, and the chilli and lime bring out the flavour beautifully.

36 fresh Knysna oysters
crushed ice

CHILLI AND LIME SORBET

(MAKES 2 LITRES)

1 litre milk

500 g sugar

500 ml lime juice

5 medium chillies, finely
    chopped

SERVES 6

The oysters Open the oysters and make sure they are clean. Set aside on a bed of crushed ice until needed.

The chilli and lime sorbet In a saucepan, bring the milk and sugar to the boil. Remove from the heat and add the lime juice and chillies. Set aside to cool, then churn in an ice-cream maker for 40 minutes.

To plate Spoon the sorbet into a small dish and place it on a bed of ice at one end of a serving platter. Arrange oysters (six per plate) over the rest of the dish.

WINE SUGGESTION

Buitenverwagting Brut

PAVILION

Carpaccio of ostrich *with a mille-feuille of rocket and Parmesan, served with a red wine vinaigrette*

How did we ever live without the healthy, cholesterol-free meat of the ostrich? The slightly bitter rocket and the Parmesan crisp give balance to the flavours.

500 g ostrich fillet

15 ml cardamom seeds, crushed

15 ml coriander seeds, crushed

15 ml black peppercorns, crushed

a small handful fresh coriander, finely chopped

zest of 1 lime

zest of 1 lemon

500 g Parmesan, grated

500 g rocket

salt to taste

100 ml red wine vinaigrette (see recipe, page 158)

SERVES 6

The ostrich Cut the fillet lengthwise into three pieces. Mix together the spices, coriander and zest, then roll the ostrich pieces in the mixture. Make sure the meat is well coated. Wrap the fillets tightly in clingfilm until they resemble sausages, and freeze for 24 hours.

The Parmesan crisps On a non-stick baking sheet, sprinkle the Parmesan in circles (5 cm in diameter) and melt under the grill. Remove from the oven and set aside to cool.

To plate Slice the ostrich into 1.5 mm-thick slices and arrange in a circle around a plate. Using alternating layers of rocket leaves and Parmesan crisps, make a tower in the middle of the plate. Season the ostrich with salt and drizzle the vinaigrette around the plate.

WINE SUGGESTION

Steenberg Merlot – 2001

PAVILION

Mediterranean vegetable terrine *with pesto*

2 large courgettes (baby
　marrows), sliced lengthwise
　into 2 mm-thick slices
2 green peppers
2 red peppers
2 yellow peppers
2 large aubergines (brinjals),
　sliced lengthwise into
　2 mm-thick slices
40 ml olive oil
salt and freshly ground black
　pepper to taste
60 ml basil pesto (see recipe,
　page 159)
5 plum tomatoes, skinned,
　seeded and quartered
6 lettuce leaves

SERVES 6

The vegetables Place the courgette slices on a baking sheet and pop under the grill until just tender. Place all the peppers on a baking sheet and bake in a preheated oven at 180 °C until the skin begins to wrinkle. Remove from the oven and, as soon as they can be handled, wrap the peppers in clingfilm. Set aside for 30 minutes to loosen the skin from the flesh, then peel and seed the peppers. Reduce the oven temperature to 160 °C. Lay the aubergine slices on a well-oiled baking sheet and bake for 5 minutes.

To assemble Brush a terrine mould with olive oil and line with clingfilm. Brush the clingfilm with olive oil. Layer the aubergine slices around the edges of the mould, season and brush with pesto. Make sure that both the clingfilm and aubergine slices overlap the edge of the terrine. Layer the peppers, grilled courgettes and tomato from the bottom up, taking care to alternate the colours of the vegetables. Fold the aubergine slices over the top of the terrine and wrap up with the clingfilm. Place the terrine on a tray in the refrigerator and place a heavy object evenly over the whole terrine to ensure even downward pressure. Leave for at least 5 hours to set.

To plate Cut the terrine into 2 cm-thick slices and place one slice on each cold plate. Arrange some dressed seasonal lettuce on the side and drizzle basil pesto around the plate.

Note: This dish is suitable for vegetarians. In the case of vegans or those with lactose intolerance, omit the Parmesan from the pesto.

WINE SUGGESTION
JC le Roux Chardonnay – 1998
or Newton Johnson Chardonnay
– 1998

This dish is simple and fresh, and the ultimate taste experience for any vegetarian. And for those who are not.

Grilled kabeljou with saffron potato cakes and tomato confit, *served with a langoustine and chardonnay velouté*

6 x 200 g portions kabeljou

salt and freshly ground black
    pepper to taste

50 g butter

6 x 40–60 g langoustines

6 x 150 g saffron potato cakes
    (see recipe, page 160)

54 julienne strips of cucumber

18 cherry tomatoes

6 sprigs fresh rosemary

50 ml olive oil

270 ml velouté (see recipe,
    page 158)

SERVES 6

The kabeljou Season the fish and seal it in a hot pan with half the butter. Transfer to a roasting pan, skin side up, and roast in a preheated oven at 180 °C for 6 minutes.

The langoustines Cut the langoustines in half and season. Fry in a non-stick pan with the remaining butter until the flesh is firm.

The accompaniments Bake the saffron potato cakes in the oven at 180 °C for 8–10 minutes until golden. Place the cucumber strips in boiling water until warmed through, then drain and season. Wrap the tomatoes in foil with the rosemary, olive oil and some seasoning and bake at 180 °C for 6–7 minutes.

To plate Place a potato cake in the centre of each plate. Arrange the tomatoes around this and place nine strips of cucumber on top of the cake. Drizzle the velouté around the plate and place the fish on top of the cucumber. Place the langoustine on top of the fish.

WINE SUGGESTION

Newton Johnson

Chardonnay – 2001

Kabeljou (kob) is undoubtedly the finest and most delicate of our South African fishes. The saffron adds a perfect fusion of flavour and colour, with the langoustine rounding off a well-balanced dish.

PAVILION

Roast fillet of beef *with cabbage parcels, sweet potato fondant, asparagus and bone marrow*

We use the best ingredients for this dish and cook them simply and well.

The sweet potato fondant Peel the potatoes and cut the sides off with a pastry cutter to form a flat disc 1 cm in diameter and 2 cm thick. Seal the potatoes in a frying pan with olive oil until both sides are golden brown. Transfer to a small roasting pan, then add the chicken stock, clarified butter and thyme. The liquid should come three-quarters of the way up the sides of the potato discs. Bake in a preheated oven at 180 °C for about 20 minutes, then remove and set aside.

The beef Seal the beef portions in a very hot griddle pan for about 1 minute each side. Season well and dress lightly with a little of the clarified butter mixture spooned off from the sweet potatoes. Roast in the oven at 180 °C for 8–10 minutes.

The asparagus Sauté the asaparagus tips in a hot pan with a little clarified butter mixture spooned off from the sweet potatoes. Season and set aside.

The cabbage parcels Remove the large outer leaves from the cabbages, then chop the smaller inner leaves. Blanche the outer leaves then refresh in ice water. Drain and roll the leaves flat with a rolling pin (cover the leaves with a clean cloth to prevent damage). Sauté the bacon, adding the chopped cabbage and onion at the last minute. Lay two overlapping cabbage leaves on a cloth, spoon one-sixth of the cabbage-bacon mixture on top, then fold over the leaves and form into a patty shape. Press down to remove excess liquid. Sauté the parcels in goose fat for 2 minutes each side over a moderate heat.

The bone marrow Slice the bone marrow into 2 mm-thick slices and sauté in a little of the goose fat. Season to taste.

To plate Place a cabbage cake in the centre of each plate, with three sweet potato fondants arranged around it. Place two asparagus tips on top of each fondant. Cut the fillet into three slices and place on top of the cabbage parcel. Spoon the jus around and garnish with bone marrow.

6 x 180 g portions beef fillet
salt and freshly ground black
  pepper to taste
18 asparagus tips, blanched
2 medium heads Savoy
  cabbage
12 rashers rindless back
  bacon, finely chopped
3 medium onions, finely
  chopped
250 ml goose fat
90 g bone marrow
80 ml port jus (see recipe,
  page 156)

SWEET POTATO FONDANT
6 medium sweet potatoes
a little olive oil
500 ml chicken stock
  (see recipe, page 152)
450 ml clarified butter
  (see recipe, page 153)
20 sprigs fresh thyme

SERVES 6

WINE SUGGESTION
Rupert and Rothschild
Classique – 2001

PAVILION

Pan-fried loin of Karoo lamb, *dauphinoise potatoes, roast garlic and onions and portabellini mushrooms with a thyme jus*

Those who've experienced the unique scents and flavours of the Karoo will know that such delicious grazing produces lamb that is among the best in the world.

6 x 180 g portions lamb loin
salt and freshly ground black
    pepper to taste
18 baby onions
12 cloves garlic
400 ml olive oil
9 medium-sized portabellini
    mushrooms, halved
60 leaves baby spinach
5 ml grated nutmeg
100 ml thyme jus (see recipe,
    page 157)

DAUPHINOISE POTATOES
6 large potatoes, peeled
1 whole nutmeg, grated
salt and freshly ground black
    pepper to taste
400 ml fresh cream

SERVES 6

WINE SUGGESTION
Hamilton Russell
Pinot Noir – 2001

The lamb Score the fat side of the lamb portions to ensure they don't curl up during cooking, and season. Lightly oil a hot pan and seal the lamb, fat side first. Set aside to rest – only finish off cooking in the oven just before serving.

The roast garlic and onions Trim and peel the onions and garlic. Place them in a saucepan, cover in olive oil and heat until bubbling. Transfer to a preheated oven at 100 °C and roast for 2 hours.

The dauphinoise potatoes Place a sheet of silicone paper at the bottom of a well-greased, deep baking sheet or roasting pan. Using a mandolin, slice the potatoes paper thin. Arrange an overlapping layer of potatoes on the silicone paper and season with nutmeg, salt and pepper. Cover with a little cream. Repeat these layers until the potatoes reach a height of 5 cm. Bake in the oven at 180 °C for 40 minutes. Remove from the oven, weight down and leave to cool, then cut out circles using a 5 cm diameter round pastry cutter. Reheat just before serving.

The mushrooms In a hot pan, sauté the mushrooms until tender, then season. Set aside.

The spinach In a very hot pan, sauté the spinach until just wilted, and season with nutmeg.

To plate Arrange three mushroom halves on the right-hand side of each plate. Place the onions and garlic on the left-hand side of the plate. Place a bed of spinach at the top of the plate and top with dauphinoise potatoes. Slice the meat and arrange it from the dauphinoise potatoes to the opposite side of the plate. Drizzle the thyme jus around the plate and serve.

Slow-roasted duck leg *with sesame and orange,* and pan-seared breast, *with basmati rice and stir-fried vegetables*

6 duck legs and thighs

24 sprigs fresh thyme

12 cloves garlic

10 ml olive oil

60 ml orange juice

20 ml sesame seeds

15 ml soy sauce

6 duck breasts

30 ml honey

30 ml duck jus (see recipe, page 157)

30 ml chilli jam (see recipe, page 154)

BASMATI RICE

1 each small red, yellow and green pepper

1 medium onion

a handful fresh coriander

300 g basmati rice

500 ml chicken stock (see recipes, page 152)

STIR-FRY VEGETABLES

1 small leek

1 medium carrot

1 large courgette (baby marrow)

30 ml butter

SERVES 6

WINE SUGGESTION

Southern Right Pinotage – 2002

The slow-roasted leg of duck Debone the duck leg and thigh, leaving only the leg bone sticking out. Place on aluminium foil and add seasoning, thyme, garlic and olive oil. Wrap up tightly, place the parcel in a roasting pan and roast in a preheated oven at 120 °C for 1 hour. Reduce the orange juice to 30 ml, then mix in the sesame seeds and soy sauce. Remove the duck from the oven, open the foil and drizzle the orange juice mixture over the duck legs. Set aside and keep warm.

The basmati rice Chop the peppers and onion and sauté until the onion is translucent. Roughly chop the coriander and mix it into the peppers and onion. Season to taste. Place the rice on a baking sheet, pour over the chicken stock and cover with foil. Bake at 160 °C for 10 minutes. Remove from the oven, remove the foil and fork in the peppers and onion mixture. Adjust seasoning, cover again with foil and bake for another 10 minutes.

The pan-seared breast of duck Season the duck breasts and seal, skin side down, in a pan. Cook in the pan until golden brown, then turn over and drizzle with honey. Set aside and keep warm.

The stir-fried vegetables Julienne the vegetables and stir-fry for a minute or two in the butter.

To plate Place the stir-fried vegetables in the centre of each plate and spoon the rice on top. Slice the breast thinly and fan out in front of the rice. Place the leg on top of the rice and spoon the duck jus around. Drizzle some chilli jam around the jus.

Two cooking methods on one plate: the usually tough leg becomes tender and nearly falls off the bone in this dish, and the breast stays moist and succulent. For anyone who's been reluctant to cook duck, this recipe is a must.

PAVILION

Roast tandoori-spiced ostrich fillet

6 x 200 g portions ostrich fillet

30 ml tandoori spice

salt and freshly ground black
   pepper to taste

42 baby potatoes, cooked and
   halved

250 ml plain yoghurt

2 cloves garlic, chopped

60 g mint, chopped

80 g mixed lettuce leaves

3 tomatoes, cut into strips

125 ml olive oil

50 ml balsamic vinegar

6 poppadums

100 ml thyme jus (see recipe,
   page 157)

SERVES 6

WINE SUGGESTION

Southern Right Pinotage – 2000

The ostrich Sprinkle the fillets with the tandoori spice and seasoning. Seal the ostrich in a very hot pan, then roast in a preheated oven at 180 °C for 5–6 minutes. Set aside to rest.

The accompaniments Blanch the baby potatoes and cool slightly, then mix them with the yoghurt, garlic and mint. Mix the lettuce and tomato together and dress with the olive oil and balsamic vinegar. Deep-fry the poppadums.

To plate Arrange the dressed potatoes around the plate with slices of the ostrich on top. Put the salad in the poppadum and place it in the centre of the plate. Spoon the thyme jus over the ostrich and serve at once.

In this dish we take the lean, fat-free meat of the ostrich and marry it with the North Indian spices, creating a meal that is both spicy and flavourful.

Roast breast of free-range chicken *on a basil and tomato tart*

6 deboned chicken breasts
(skin on)
salt and freshly ground black
pepper to taste
90 ml olive oil
1 x 250 g tub mascarpone
cheese
a small bunch chives, snipped
90 ml tomato salsa (see recipe,
page 161)

BASIL AND TOMATO TART
600 g ready-made puff pastry
6 large, ripe plum tomatoes
48 fresh basil leaves
salt and freshly ground black
pepper to taste
90 ml basil pesto (see recipe,
page 159)
50 g Parmesan, grated

SERVES 6

WINE SUGGESTION
Hamilton Russel
Chardonnay – 2002

The basil and tomato tart Roll out the pastry on a lightly floured surface to 2 mm thick. Cut out six rounds measuring 12 cm in diameter (use a small plate or saucer as a guide). Place the rounds on a baking sheet and chill for 20 minutes. Bake in a preheated oven at 200 °C for 10 minutes, then place another baking sheet on top of the pastry and bake for a further 8 minutes. Place the discs on a wire rack to cool. Slice the tomatoes evenly and arrange the slices, alternating with basil leaves, on top of the pastry discs. Season lightly and drizzle with basil pesto. Sprinkle over the Parmesan. Just before serving, place the tarts in the oven until the cheese melts and turns golden brown.

The chicken Season the breasts well, then sear in a non-stick frying pan in the olive oil. Transfer to a roasting pan and roast at 200 °C for 10 minutes.

The mascarpone cheese Mix the cheese and chives, and add seasoning.

To plate Place a tart in the centre of each plate. Cut the chicken breasts in half, at a slant, and arrange on top of the tart. Spoon some tomato salsa around the tart and place a dollop of the mascarpone and chive mixture on top of each chicken breast.

This is a lesson in simplicity: chicken, tomato and basil, a fresh, light and healthy dish with loads of flavour.

Summer garden lasagne

The vegetables Blanch the patty pans, carrots and asparagus in boiling water, then refresh in ice water. Sauté in a pan with the butter, adding the peas, mushrooms and bean sprouts at the last minute.

The lasagne Blanch the lasagne sheets in boiling water, then remove and toss in a non-stick pan with some olive oil and seasoning until *al dente*.

The beetroot Cook the beetroot in boiling, salted water until soft. When cool enough to handle, peel and quarter the beetroot, then toss in a hot pan with some olive oil. Remove from the heat and add the honey. Set aside.

The watercress cream Bring the cream to the boil, then reduce it by half and add the watercress and seasoning. Pour into a blender and blend until smooth.

The mascarpone cheese Mix the cheese and chives, and add seasoning.

To plate Place a sheet of lasagne in the bottom of each pasta bowl. Spoon half the vegetables, excluding the beetroot, on top, then repeat the process, ending with a sheet of lasagne. Pour the watercress cream around the bowl. Spoon the beetroot on top of the lasagne and top this with some mascarpone cheese. Drizzle with beetroot juices.

A symphony of mushrooms, baby vegetables, peas and sprouts on a light watercress cream.

24 yellow patty pans, quartered
24 baby carrots, halved
  lengthwise
36 fresh asparagus spears,
  halved lengthwise
60 g butter
150 g frozen peas
18 portabellini mushrooms,
  quartered
18 oyster mushrooms,
  quartered
150 g bean sprouts
18 sheets lasagne
60 ml olive oil
salt and freshly ground black
  pepper to taste
6 baby beetroot
100 ml honey
180 ml fresh cream
180 g watercress
60 g mascarpone cheese
a small bunch chives, snipped

SERVES 6

WINE SUGGESTION
Hamilton Russell
Chardonnay – 1999

PAVILION

Dark chocolate-raisin parfait *with brandy sauce*

The parfait Whisk the egg yolks and the castor sugar until light and fluffy. In a separate bowl, whip the cream until stiff. Fold the cream and the melted chocolate into the egg and sugar mixture, then add the raisins. Pour into six individual moulds and freeze for 4 hours.

The brandy sauce Heat the cream in a saucepan over a low heat. In a separate bowl, whisk the egg yolks and castor sugar until light in colour. Pour the warm cream into the egg mixture and whisk until the sugar has dissolved. Strain into a clean bowl. Stir the mixture over a double-boiler until it starts to thicken. The mixture is cooked when it coats the back of a spoon. Stir in the brandy.

To plate Drizzle the brandy sauce over each plate. Unmould the parfaits onto the centre. Decorate with mixed berries, a sprig of mint and a chocolate cigar.

Brandy, raisins and chocolate provide a light finish to a meal. This parfait is suitable for a beautiful summer's evening, as well as a cold winter's night.

PARFAIT

5 egg yolks
125 g castor sugar
500 ml fresh cream
120 g dark Callebaut Belgian
    chocolate, melted
50 g seedless raisins

BRANDY SAUCE

250 ml fresh cream
3 egg yolks
60 g castor sugar
30 ml brandy

DECORATION

mixed berries
fresh mint
chocolate cigar

SERVES 6

WINE SUGGESTION
Graham Beck Rhona
White Muscadel – 1998

PAVILION

Coffee crème brûlée *with chocolate and mixed nut biscotti*

CHOCOLATE AND MIXED
NUT BISCOTTI

60 g soft butter

150 g brown sugar

1 egg

215 g cake flour

125 g mixed nuts, roughly
     chopped

80 g dark chocolate, roughly
     chopped

5 ml baking powder

COFFEE CRÈME BRÛLÉE

225 ml milk

750 ml fresh cream

50 g coffee beans

10 egg yolks

140 g castor sugar

SERVES 6

The chocolate and mixed nut biscotti Mix the butter and sugar until light and fluffy, then whisk in the egg. Fold in the flour, nuts, chocolate and baking powder until a pliable dough forms. Shape the dough into a cylinder, wrap it in clingfilm and leave to rest in the refrigerator for 1 hour. Slice the dough into 5 mm-thick discs and arrange on a non-stick baking sheet. Bake in a preheated oven at 180 °C for 10 minutes or until golden brown. Cool on a wire rack.

The coffee crème brûlée In a saucepan, bring the milk, cream and coffee beans to the boil. In a bowl, make a paste with the egg yolks and sugar. Add the milk mixture to the paste, stirring, then set aside for 1 hour to cool. Strain the beans, then pour the liquid into six coffee cups. Place the cups in a *bain-marie* and bake in the oven at 100 °C for 40 minutes.

To plate Sprinkle some brown sugar on top of the crème brûlées, then caramelize the sugar with a blowtorch or under the grill. Place the cup on the saucer, with the biscotti on the side.

WINE SUGGESTION

Walker Bay Beaumont
Goutte d'Or – 2001

This rich, smooth-textured dessert is known as 'burnt cream' in England, where it has been popular since the 17th century. It was not until the late 1800s, however, that the French name became popular.

Raspberry and peach soufflé *with vanilla yoghurt ice cream*

VANILLA YOGHURT
ICE CREAM

(MAKES 1 LITRE)
500 ml milk
1 vanilla pod
6 egg yolks
200 g sugar
500 ml fresh cream
500 ml plain yoghurt

RASPBERRY AND
PEACH SOUFFLÉ
clarified butter for brushing
   (see recipe, page 153)
castor sugar for dusting
60 g raspberries
60 g peaches, peeled and
   stoned
100 g castor sugar
4 egg whites

DECORATION
fresh raspberries
fresh mint
raspberry coulis (see recipe for
   raspberry coulis, page 161)

SERVES 6

WINE SUGGESTION
Walker Bay Beaumont
Goutte d'Or – 2001

The vanilla yoghurt ice cream In a saucepan, bring the milk and vanilla pod to the boil. In a bowl, mix the egg yolks and sugar to form a paste. Remove the milk from the heat, discard the vanilla pod and add the milk to the egg paste. Whisk well. Leave the mixture to cool to room temperature, then add the cream and yoghurt. Pour the mixture into an ice-cream maker and churn for 40 minutes.

The raspberry and peach soufflé Brush six ramekins with clarified butter and dust with a little castor sugar. Place the raspberries and peaches in a blender and blend until smooth. Pour the fruit purée into a saucepan, add 40 g of the castor sugar and cook over a low heat for about 5 minutes. Whisk the egg whites and remaining sugar until light and fluffy. Fold the hot raspberry mixture into the egg whites, then spoon the mixture into a piping bag and pipe it into the ramekins. Bake in a preheated oven at 180 °C for 15–20 minutes.

To plate Place a soufflé on the left-hand side of each plate, and serve the ice cream on the right-hand side. Decorate with raspberries, mint and raspberry coulis.

The French word soufflé means to puff or to blow up. Unfortunately, a soufflé has the bad reputation of being difficult to make, but this version is simple.

PAVILION

Sticky date and chocolate pudding *with mocha ice cream*

The pudding In a heavy-based saucepan, boil the jam and dates in the water for 10–15 minutes until the dates are soft. Remove from the heat and add the chocolate. In a mixing bowl, cream the butter and the sugar. Add the eggs, egg yolks and vanilla essence, then mix in the flour. Stir the date mixture into the flour mixture. Pour the mixture into six ramekins, then place these in a *bain-marie* and bake in a preheated oven at 100 °C for 45 minutes.

The mocha ice cream In a saucepan, bring the milk and coffee beans to the boil. Add the chocolate. In a bowl, mix the egg yolks and sugar to form a paste. Remove the milk from the heat and add to the egg paste, whisking well. Leave the mixture to cool to room temperature, then add the cream. Pour the mixture into an ice-cream maker and churn for 40 minutes.

To plate Unmould the puddings on the left-hand side of each plate. Serve the ice cream in a tuile basket (see recipe, page 162) alongside and drizzle chocolate sauce (see recipe, page 162) all round.

This is our contribution to a classic dessert, with the addition of plum jam to further enhance the flavour.

PUDDING

250 g plum jam

450 g stoned dates, finely chopped

450 ml water

300 g dark Callebaut Belgian chocolate, roughly broken

200 g butter

375 g sugar

3 eggs

3 egg yolks

5 ml vanilla essence

300 g self-raising flour

MOCHA ICE CREAM

(MAKES 1 LITRE)

500 ml milk

60 g coffee beans

60 g dark Callebaut Belgian chocolate

6 egg yolks

200 g sugar

500 ml fresh cream

SERVES 6

WINE SUGGESTION

Graham Beck Rhona
White Muscadel – 1998

PAVILION

'Torta' of strawberries *with mint cream and balsamic ice cream*

100 g strawberries, halved
strawberry jam

BALSAMIC ICE CREAM
(MAKES 1 LITRE)
300 ml balsamic vinegar
500 ml milk
6 egg yolks
200 g sugar
500 ml fresh cream

MINT CREAM
200 ml fresh cream
a small handful fresh mint,
    chopped

CRÊPE BATTER
180 ml milk
40 ml butter, melted
80 g cake flour
25 ml sugar
2.5 ml salt
3 eggs
5 ml vanilla essence

SERVES 6

WINE SUGGESTION
Graham Beck Rhona
White Muscadel – 1998

The balsamic ice cream In a saucepan, bring the balsamic vinegar to the boil and reduce by half. In a separate saucepan, bring the milk to the boil. In a bowl, mix the egg yolks and sugar to form a paste. Remove the milk from the heat and add it the egg paste, whisking well. Leave the mixture to cool to room temperature, then add the cream and balsamic reduction. Pour the mixture into an ice-cream maker and churn for 40 minutes.

The mint cream Whip the cream until soft peaks form, then fold in the mint.

The crêpes Warm the milk and butter in a saucepan over a moderate heat. In a mixing bowl, mix together the flour, sugar, salt and eggs. Add the vanilla essence to the milk and butter mixture, then mix this into the flour mixture until smooth. Heat a non-stick frying pan, then pour in a little batter. Swirl the batter in the pan so that it just covers the base. Fry until golden, then turn over and fry the other side. Remove the crêpe and set aside. Repeat with the remaining batter (you will need 18 crêpes).

To plate Cut the crêpes with a 6 cm diameter round pastry cutter. Place a crêpe on each plate, spread with jam and top with strawberries. Repeat the process twice more, ending with a crêpe. Top with a scoop of mint cream and serve the ice cream alongside.

Balsamic vinegar and mint bring out the flavour of South African strawberries. The ice cream is a perfect accompaniment to this unusual fusion of pancakes and strawberries.

PAVILION

Wild honey parfait with fresh strawberries *in balsamic syrup*

A parfait is a delicate frozen dessert, usually lighter and less sweet than ice cream, made from a mixture of egg yolks and sugar, with whipped cream and flavouring. Definitely not for the calorie conscious!

18 strawberries, halved

PARFAIT
5 egg yolks
125 g castor sugar
500 ml fresh cream
50 ml wild honey

BALSAMIC SYRUP
250 ml balsamic vinegar
250 ml water
500 g sugar

DECORATION
sprigs fresh mint

SERVES 4

The parfait Whisk the egg yolks and castor sugar until light and fluffy. Whip the cream until stiff peaks form, then fold the cream and the honey into the egg and sugar mixture. Pour into eight individual moulds and freeze for 4 hours.

The balsamic syrup Place all the ingredients in a heavy-based saucepan and cook over a low heat for about 1 hour, until reduced to a thick syrup consistency.

To plate Unmould the parfaits and place two, one on top of the other, on the left of each plate. Arrange the strawberries on the right-hand side. Spoon droplets of balsamic syrup on the edge of the plate and decorate with mint.

WINE SUGGESTION
Graham Beck Rhona White
Muscadel – 1998

Liz McGrath's inspiration for Seafood at The Marine came about

after a chance visit to the seafood counter at Harrods in London.

Seafood is a bright restaurant in the modern idiom, where the

only view of the sea is on the plate.

The style is informal and busy, with the emphasis on the

freshness of the fish from Walker Bay, great style and friendly

service. The open kitchen, with its all-girl team of chefs, provides

diners with a close-up view of the frenetic activity.

SEAFOOD
AT THE MARINE ～ HERMANUS

RUMÉ BOOYSENS – **Chef de Cuisine**

After training at the Christina Martin School of Food and Wine in Durban, Rumé joined the bustling kitchen of Stephanie's in Sandton, at which time Johannesburg's restaurants started a trend now referred to as contemporary South African cuisine.

Rumé broadened her experience in Europe, before returning to South Africa to take up her post at The Marine in 1999. Since then, she has taken Seafood at the Marine to great heights, accumulating numerous awards, including a Top 100 rating by *Wine* magazine for her interpretation of classic dishes with a distinctly South African feel.

Rumé's philosophy on food is that it should reflect flare, control and discipline, combined with a touch of frenzied passion.

Marine seafood *soup*

Seafood soup has been a consistent item on the menu for over two seasons and is a favourite of many guests. The dish is served as a starter, but a larger portion will do just as well as a main course.

250 g fish bones

1 carrot

1 onion

1 stick celery

1 leek

2 tomatoes

a handful fennel

1 clove garlic

1 cm piece fresh root ginger

50 ml dry white wine

15 ml tomato paste

water to cover

a pinch of saffron

a pinch of cayenne pepper

salt and freshly ground black
pepper to taste

GARNISH

olive oil to drizzle

chopped fresh parsley

rouille

SERVES 4–6

The soup In a large, heavy-based saucepan, fry the bones in a little oil over a moderate heat until cooked. Add the vegetables, fennel, garlic and ginger and sauté for another 10 minutes. Deglaze with white wine and tomato paste, then add water to cover. Allow to boil for at least 3 hours, keeping the water level constant. Pour the soup into a blender and blend until the bones are completely broken up. Strain through a fine sieve. While the soup is still hot, add the saffron, cayenne pepper and seasoning, and leave the saffron to infuse for at least 30 minutes before serving.

WINE SUGGESTION

Buitenverwachting
Blanc de Noir – 2001

To plate Reheat the soup and ladle into soup bowls. Finish off with olive oil and chopped parsley. If desired, serve the soup with a mussel and a piece of line fish to give the dish some texture.

SEAFOOD
AT THE MARINE ━ HERMANUS

Traditional fish cakes

Usually hake doesn't inspire the tastebuds, but this recipe uses its unique texture and flavour to create a simple yet delicious dish.

1 kg hake fillets
a bunch spring onions, finely
   chopped
1 fresh red chilli, chopped
100 ml mayonnaise
5 ml Tabasco sauce
15 ml Worcestershire sauce
salt and freshly ground black
   pepper to taste
90 ml cake flour
1 egg, beaten
50 g dried breadcrumbs

GARNISH
fresh dill

SERVES 6

The fish cakes Grill the hake for 3 minutes each side until flaky, then drain it until the flesh is totally dry. Flake the fish and combine with the spring onions, chilli, mayonnaise, Tabasco and Worcestershire sauce. Add seasoning. Shape the mixture into little round cakes of about 65 g each. Dust the cakes with flour, dip in the beaten egg and cover with breadcrumbs. Chill in the refrigerator for about 30 minutes to set. Fry off when needed.

To plate Serve with a green salad, lemon wedges, tartare sauce (see recipe, page 155) and tomato salsa (see recipe, page 161). Place the salad on one side of the plate with the fish cake at the other side of the plate. Serve the tartare sauce and tomato salsa in butter dishes alongside, with lemon wedges in between.

WINE SUGGESTION
Southern Right
Sauvignon Blanc – 2002

Ravioli *of prawns and creamed leeks*

RAVIOLI

2 large leeks, finely chopped

500 ml fresh cream

salt and freshly ground black
    pepper to taste

6 tiger prawns, peeled

24 wonton sheets

1 egg, beaten

VINAIGRETTE

300 ml seafood soup
    (see recipe, page 130)

10 ml olive oil

10 ml balsamic vinegar

SERVES 4

The ravioli Blanch the leeks in boiling, salted water for a few seconds. In a saucepan, reduce the cream to about 100 ml, then add it to the leeks, and season. Cut the prawns into four pieces each. Spoon a little of the creamed leeks onto each wonton pastry and top with a piece of prawn. Brush the edges of the pastry with egg and fold into a triangle. Cook in simmering water for 3 minutes.

The vinaigrette Strain the soup into a clean saucepan and reduce to about 150 ml. Leave to cool, then add the olive oil and balsamic vinegar and mix well.

To plate Fan the ravioli on a plate and dress with the vinaigrette. If desired, serve with a salad of rocket and Parmesan, which not only gives good colour to this dish, but is also a light addition that does not overpower the flavour.

This dish is a perfect item on any menu as it is suitable for any season. It is light enough for a main course in the summer and a favourite as a starter during the colder months.

WINE SUGGESTION

Haute Cabrière
Chardonnay – 2001

SeaFood
AT THE MARINE · HERMANUS

Marine Caesar salad

The salad Cut the baguette into 1 cm cubes and season with thyme, olive oil, salt and pepper. Place on a baking sheet and toast under the grill until golden brown. On a piece of greaseproof paper, arrange the grated Parmesan in 7 cm diameter circles and melt under the grill until it starts to bubble. Set aside to cool until crisp. Chop the bacon into 1 cm pieces. Wash and dry the lettuce.

The dressing Whisk the egg yolks and water until light and fluffy. Add the anchovies and whisk until blended. Mix in the vinegar and lemon juice. Slowly add the oil, whisking continuously until all the oil has been added. Add the garlic and seasoning.

To plate Assemble all the salad ingredients, except the Parmesan crisps, in a bowl. Dress with the anchovy dressing and garnish with a Parmesan crisp.

1 small baguette
4 sprigs fresh thyme, leaves
    removed and stems
    discarded
20 ml olive oil
salt and freshly ground black
    pepper to taste
100 g Parmesan, grated
500 g bacon, fried until crispy
6 heads cos lettuce

DRESSING

3 egg yolks
80 ml water
50 g can anchovies, finely
    chopped
30 ml white wine vinegar
juice of 1 lemon
250 ml vegetable oil
5 ml crushed garlic
salt and freshly ground black
    pepper to taste

SERVES 6

As the trend towards lighter eating continues, salads are becoming increasingly popular as a main course.

WINE SUGGESTION

Hamilton Russell
Chardonnay – 1999

Rich man's fish and chips

With this classic dish it is absolutely vital that you use the freshest ingredients, and that includes the oil for frying.

2 kg hake

250 g cornflour

270 g cake flour

50 ml baking powder

salt and freshly ground black
  pepper to taste

90 ml water

90 ml milk

1.2 kg potatoes

oil for deep-frying

SERVES 6

The fish Clean and debone the hake and cut it into portions, or ask your fishmonger to do it for you. Mix together the dry ingredients, then whisk in the water and milk until combined. Make sure there are no lumps. Dust the hake with flour and dip into the batter. Allow excess batter to drip off. Fry in a deep-fryer preheated to 140 °C for 3–4 minutes. Remove and place on kitchen paper to drain excess oil.

The chips Peel the potatoes and cut them into chips. Deep-fry in hot oil until golden. Remove and place on kitchen paper to drain excess oil.

To plate Place the fish in the centre of the plate with the chips wrapped in a paper cone alongside. Serve tartare sauce (see recipe, page 155) and tomato salsa (see recipe, page 161) in butter dishes on the other side of the fish.

WINE SUGGESTION

Klein Constantia
Chardonnay – 2001

SEAFOOD

Grilled Walker Bay sole

The Atlantic Ocean may not be famous for its warm water, but it certainly is well known for the quality of sole that it produces. This dish is an all-time favourite, and is so simple to prepare.

The fish Pat the soles dry with kitchen paper and season with salt, pepper and lemon juice. Seal in a griddle pan large enough to accommodate the whole sole, then transfer to a roasting pan and roast in a preheated oven at 180 °C for about 4 minutes.

The vegetables Bake the dauphinoise potatoes at 180 °C for 6 minutes. Sauté all the vegetables in a little butter and olive oil, and season to taste.

To plate Gently place the sole at an angle on an oval plate with the potatoes at the tail end of the sole and the vegetables half under and to the side of the sole. Spoon the sauce verge around the sole and serve with two wedges of lemon per plate. Garnish with coriander.

6 x 450 g soles, trimmed and
  skinned
salt and white pepper to taste
20 ml lemon juice
6 x 80 g portions dauphinoise
  potatoes (see recipe,
  page 106)
60 g English spinach
60 g broccoli
60 g bok choy
30 g courgette (baby marrow),
  julienned
10 ml butter
20 ml olive oil
120 ml sauce verge
  (see recipe, page 158)
12 lemon wedges

GARNISH
fresh coriander

SERVES 6

WINE SUGGESTION
Hamilton Russell
Chardonnay – 1999

Line fish *with red pepper sauce, polenta chips, ratatouille and rocket foam*

6 x 200 g portions line fish
salt and white pepper to taste
10 ml butter
6 red peppers

POLENTA

500 g polenta
250 ml milk
250 ml fresh cream
125 g Parmesan, grated
a bunch spring onions, chopped
a handful fresh basil, chopped
2 small red chillies, chopped
200 g cake flour

RATATOUILLE

½ red pepper
½ yellow pepper
½ green pepper
½ small aubergine (brinjal)
1 courgette (baby marrow)
1 medium onion
1 tomato, skinned
10 ml olive oil
20 ml basil pesto

ROCKET FOAM

100 ml low-fat milk
40 g rocket

SERVES 6

WINE SUGGESTION

Hamilton Russell
Chardonnay – 1999

The fish Season the fish well and seal on both sides in a very hot pan in the butter. Transfer to a roasting pan and roast in a preheated oven at 180 °C for about 8 minutes.

The red pepper sauce Place the peppers in a roasting pan and roast at 180 °C until the skins start to wrinkle. Remove the peppers from the oven and wrap in clingfilm. When cool enough to handle, peel and seed them. Cut the peppers into rough cubes, place in a blender and blend until smooth. Transfer to a saucepan and reduce the purée over a high heat to a sauce consistency.

The polenta In a separate saucepan, cook the polenta in half the milk and all the cream for 12–15 minutes until just firm. If it firms up too much, add a little hot water. Stir in the remaining ingredients, except the flour, and season with salt and black pepper to taste. Transfer to a 2 cm-deep tray, smooth the surface and leave to set in the refrigerator. Once set, cut the polenta in 2 x 6 cm chips. Dip the chips into the leftover milk, dust with flour and deep-fry until crisp.

The ratatouille Dice all the vegetables. Heat the olive oil in a large, heavy-based pan and sauté all the vegetables, adding the pesto at the last minute.

The rocket foam Bring the low-fat milk to the boil, add salt to taste, then add the rocket. Pour the mixture into a blender and blend until the rocket is infused and the foam is a bright green colour.

To plate Drizzle the red pepper sauce over the plate and place a polenta chip in the centre. Place a spoonful of ratatouille on both sides of the polenta chip. Arrange the fish on top of the polenta chip and spoon the foam over the fish. Serve at once.

This Mediterranean-inspired dish is fresh and exciting to eat.

Bunny chow

SEAFOOD CURRY

3 large onions, finely chopped
5 ml crushed garlic
5 ml crushed coriander seeds
5 ml cumin seeds
5 ml garam masala
5 ml turmeric
5 ml cayenne pepper
5 ml leaf masala
5 ml mild curry powder
2 cardamom pods
2 bay leaves
2.5 ml ground cloves
1 stick cinnamon
1 kg English tomatoes, chopped
100 ml water
½ x 410 g can coconut milk
900 g line fish
18 whole mussels
480 g calamari tubes
12 medium to large prawns
12 patti pans, quartered
12 courgettes (baby marrows), roughly sliced
54 fine green beans, topped, tailed and halved
18 leaves bok choy, halved lengthwise

FLOWERPOT BREAD

(MAKES 6 SMALL BREADS)

15 ml honey
20 g fresh yeast
300 ml lukewarm water
900 g cake flour
20 ml salt

SERVES 6

The seafood curry In a large, heavy-based saucepan, fry the onions, then add the garlic and all the spices and fry for a further 5 minutes. Add the tomatoes and water and cook for about 30 minutes. Stir in the coconut milk, then add all the seafood. Cook gently for 5 minutes, then add the vegetables and cook a further 2 minutes. Discard any mussels that have not opened.

The flowerpot bread Dissolve the honey and yeast in the water, and leave to stand for a few minutes to activate the yeast. Mix the yeast mixture with the flour and salt and knead until it forms a dough. Cover with a damp cloth and leave to prove in a warm place until doubled in size. Knock down the dough. Grease six 10 cm diameter, 7 cm deep terracotta flowerpots with butter and dust with flour. Divide the dough between the pots and bake in a preheated oven at 180 °C for 20 minutes.

To plate Hollow out the bread and spoon the cooked curry inside. If desired, serve with rice on the side.

Traditionally, this dish would be served with a more spicy Indian curry, but we use this delicious Cape Malay seafood curry instead, and serve it in home-made bread baked in a flowerpot.

WINE SUGGESTION
Zandvliet Shiraz – 1999

Stir-fried calamari

Calamari lends itself well to stir-fries and with the addition of a few spices it can be turned into an exceptional dish that is ideal for entertaining at home – simple and delicious.

6 carrots

2 leeks

1 large red onion

100 g oyster mushrooms

¼ head Chinese cabbage

1 head bok choy

¼ head broccoli

250 g fine green beans

250 g mangetout (snow peas)

a little sunflower oil

100 g bean sprouts

30 ml soy sauce

30 ml oyster sauce

10 ml sesame seed oil

500 g egg noodles

1.5 kg baby calamari tubes

10 ml Chinese five spice

10 ml turmeric

salt and freshly ground black
   pepper to taste

a small handful fresh coriander
   (optional)

60 ml chilli jam (see recipe,
   page 154) (optional)

SERVES 6

WINE SUGGESTION

Groote Post Chenin Blanc – 2002

The vegetables Julienne the carrots, and slice the leeks, onion, mushrooms, cabbage and bok choy into fine strips. Cut the broccoli into small florets. Top and tail the beans and mangetout. Stir-fry the vegetables in a little oil in a smoking-hot wok until tender but still crunchy, adding the bean sprouts at the last minute. Add the soy sauce, oyster sauce and sesame seed oil, then remove from the heat and set aside.

The noodles Cook the noodles in boiling, salted water for 4–5 minutes. Cool off in ice water, then toss the noodles with the cooked vegetables to warm them.

The calamari Toss the calamari with the five spice, turmeric and seasoning and cook in a smoking hot wok in a little oil for 1–2 minutes.

To plate Serve the calamari on top of the noodles and vegetables. If preferred, top with fresh coriander and a dollop of chilli jam.

Grilled crayfish *with peppadew butter, sautéed baby potatoes and roasted asparagus*

6 whole crayfish tails
2 litres seawater
salt and freshly ground black
    pepper to taste
500 g baby potatoes
50 g butter
a handful fresh parsley,
    chopped
48 spears green asparagus
30 ml olive oil

PEPPADEW BUTTER

80 g peppadews, finely
    chopped
200 g butter, softened
salt and freshly ground black
    pepper to taste

SERVES 6

The crayfish Blanch the crayfish for 5 minutes in the boiling seawater (use salted water if seawater isn't available). Butterfly the crayfish and clean the heads. Rub the flesh with olive oil and place under the grill for 1–2 minutes. Add seasoning, then transfer to a preheated oven at 180 °C and roast for 5 minutes.

The Peppadew butter Mix the peppadews into the butter, season and roll in clingfilm. Leave to set in the refrigerator for 20 minutes.

The baby potatoes Cook the baby potatoes in boiling, salted water for about 10 minutes. Remove, drain and sauté the potatoes in the 50 g butter until golden. Sprinkle with parsley just before serving.

The asparagus Blanch the asparagus in boiling, salted water for 1 minute, then refresh in ice water. Season and roast in the oven with the olive oil for 2 minutes.

To plate Arrange the potatoes in the centre of each plate and top with eight asparagus spears. Place the crayfish on top and dot with peppadew butter.

WINE SUGGESTION

Beaumont Chardonnay – 2000

Grilled tiger prawns *with stir-fried vegetables*

3 kg tiger prawns

6 blades fresh lemon grass

salt and freshly ground black
  pepper to taste

STIR-FRY VEGETABLES

6 carrots

8 courgettes (baby marrows)

2 leeks

¼ head Chinese cabbage

1 large red onion

100 g oyster mushrooms

1 head bok choy

¼ head broccoli

250 g fine green beans

250 g mangetout (snow peas)

a little sunflower oil

100 g bean sprouts

10 ml sesame seed oil

30 ml soy sauce

30 ml oyster sauce

GARNISH

chilli jam (see recipe,
  page 154)

fresh coriander

SERVES 6

WINE SUGGESTION

Bouchard Finlayson Chardonnay
Sans Barrique – 2001

The stir-fry vegetables Cut the carrots, courgettes, leeks, cabbage, onion, mushrooms and bok choy into fine strips. Cut the broccoli into small florets. Top and tail the beans and mangetout. Stir-fry the vegetables in a little oil in a very hot wok until tender but still crunchy. Add the bean sprouts at the last minute, then season with the sesame seed oil, soy sauce and oyster sauce.

The prawns Shell the prawns, leaving only the end segment and tail. Clean well. Cut the lemon grass into 12 cm lengths and sharpen one end. Skewer four prawns onto each blade of lemon grass and season well. Fry in a very hot pan, sealing on all sides.

To plate Spoon the vegetables into the centre of the plate and top with a prawn skewer. Serve with basmati rice garnished with fresh coriander, and chilli jam for dipping.

Everyone loves prawns, but not everyone knows how to cook them. This dish proves once again that less can be more.

SeaFood
AT THE MARINE — HERMANUS

Our famous crème brûlée

The crème brûlée Heat the cream and milk together with the vanilla pod, but don't let it boil. Strain through a fine sieve. In a mixing bowl, whisk the sugar and egg yolks until light and thick. Add the hot cream mixture to the sugar-egg mixture and whisk well. Pass through a fine sieve. Pour into six ramekins, place in a *bain-marie* and bake in a preheated oven at 100 °C for 10–15 minutes until set.

To plate Sprinkle brown sugar over the crème brûlées and caramelize with a blowtorch or under the grill. Serve topped with strawberries and a sprig of mint.

750 ml fresh cream
250 ml milk
1 vanilla pod, split lengthwise
190 g sugar
10 egg yolks
brown sugar

DECORATION
fresh strawberries
fresh mint

SERVES 6

It has been said that the quality of a restaurant's crème brûlée is a good indication of the quality of its food as a whole. Crème brûlée provides a perfect end to any meal, and is a proud part of the Seafood menu.

WINE SUGGESTION
Walker Bay Beaumont
Goutte d'Or – 2002

Raspberry shortcake *with cheesecake ice cream*

SHORTCAKE

350 g unsalted butter, softened
85 g icing sugar
10 ml vanilla essence
170 g white bread flour
85 g cake flour
a pinch of salt

RASPBERRY FILLING

50 g castor sugar
60 ml water
juice of 1 lemon
500 g raspberries

CHEESECAKE ICE CREAM

(MAKES 1 LITRE)
500 ml milk
½ vanilla pod
6 egg yolks
200 g sugar
500 ml cream
500 ml smooth cottage cheese

DECORATION

3 kiwi fruit, peeled and puréed
   with icing sugar to taste
6 sprigs fresh mint

SERVES 6

WINE SUGGESTION

Slanghoek Natural Sweet – 2002

The shortcake Beat together 250 g of the butter, the icing sugar and vanilla essence until creamy. Sift the flours and salt together and fold into the butter mixture. Rest in the refrigerator for 25 minutes. Roll out the mixture on a lightly floured baking sheet to 5 mm thick. Place in a preheated oven at 180 °C and bake for about 8 minutes until golden brown. Cool on a wire rack. Melt the remaining butter. Crumble the shortcake into the butter and mix together with your hands. Roll out again to 5 mm thick and, using a saucer as a guide, cut into circles about 12 cm in diameter. Leave to set in the refrigerator for about 20 minutes.

The raspberry filling In a saucepan (off the heat), dissolve the sugar in the water. Add the lemon juice and place the saucepan on the stove. Bring to the boil, then add half the raspberries and simmer for 10 minutes over a low heat. Remove from the heat and pass through a fine sieve.

The cheesecake ice cream In a saucepan, bring the milk and vanilla pod to the boil. Mix together the egg yolks and sugar until they form a paste. Remove the milk from the heat, discard the vanilla pod and add the milk to the egg paste. Stir well. Cool the mixture to room temperature, then add the cream and cottage cheese. Churn the mixture in an ice-cream maker for 40 minutes.

To plate Arrange the remaining raspberries around the shortcake circles. Pour the raspberry filling into the centre and place a scoop of ice cream on top. Place on one side of a chilled plate and dot the kiwi fruit coulis and any leftover raspberry filling around the shortcake. Garnish with a sprig of mint.

This modern version of a raspberry cheesecake has a crunchier texture and the smoothest, creamiest ice cream.

Trio of summer sorbets

Nothing compares to the flavour of a home-made sorbet – light, refreshing and truly delicious.

ORANGE SORBET

(MAKES 2 LITRES)
750–800 g sugar
800 ml water
1.2 litres orange juice

MELON SORBET

(MAKES 2 LITRES)
700 g sugar
500 ml water
2 litres melon purée

LEMON SORBET

(MAKES 2 LITRES)
500 g sugar
1 litre milk
1 litre lemon juice

DECORATION
sprigs fresh mint

SERVES 6

The orange sorbet Dissolve the sugar in the water, then mix in the orange juice. Chill and then churn in an ice-cream maker for about 30 minutes.

The melon sorbet In a heavy-based saucepan, dissolve the sugar in the water over a high heat until it reaches a syrup consistency. Set aside. Once cooled, add the melon purée, then chill and churn in an ice-cream maker for 30 minutes.

The lemon sorbet In a heavy-based saucepan, bring the sugar and milk to the boil, stirring until the sugar has dissolved. Add the lemon juice. Chill and then churn in an ice-cream maker for about 30 minutes.

To plate Place one scoop of each sorbet in a glass and top with a sprig of mint.

WINE SUGGESTION
Buitenverwachting Rhine
Riesling – 2002

SEAFOOD
AT THE MARINE ~ HERMANUS

THE

BASICS

The Greenhouse's brown chicken stock

3 kg chicken bones, chopped

vegetable oil for roasting

6 litres water

3 sticks celery, chopped

2 large carrots, chopped

1 onion, chopped

1 leek, chopped

12 cloves garlic, crushed

a small handful fresh thyme

Place the bones in a roasting pan and roast with a little vegetable oil in the oven until golden brown. Remove and set aside. Place the remaining ingredients in the pan and roast until golden brown. Place the chicken bones and vegetables in a large saucepan. Skim off any excess fat from the roasting pan and add a little water to the juices. Bring to the boil until all the residue has been removed, then add this to the bones. Add more water to cover. Bring to the boil, then reduce the heat and simmer for 4–5 hours, skimming off excess fat from time to time. Pass through a fine sieve, then heat in a pan until reduced to 2 litres. Leave to cool, then refrigerate or freeze. MAKES 2 LITRES

The Pavilion's chicken stock

10 whole chicken carcasses

5 litres water

4 bay leaves

2 small onions, chopped

2 small leeks, chopped

4 sticks celery, chopped

500 ml dry white wine

In a large saucepan, cover the chicken carcasses with water and bring to the boil. Add the bay leaves. Reduce the heat and simmer for 2 hours. Skim off the fat and any impurities every 30 minutes. Strain through a fine sieve. In a separate saucepan, sweat the vegetables. Add the wine and reduce by half. Add the chicken stock and reduce again by half. Strain again. The stock can be stored in the refrigerator for up to a week, and can also be frozen. MAKES 800 ML

Fish stock

1 large onion, chopped

a large handful parsley stalks

a bunch celery, chopped

400 g fish bones

2 litres water

In a large saucepan, sweat the onions, parsley and celery, then add the fish bones and water. Simmer for 45 minutes, then strain. The stock will keep in the refrigerator for up to a week, and can also be frozen. MAKES 2 LITRES

Vegetable stock

Roughly chop all the vegetables, then place them in a saucepan and cover with water. Add the peppercorns and star anise. Bring to the boil, then reduce the heat and simmer for 20 minutes. Remove from the heat, add the lemon slices and wine and cover the pan with clingfilm. Leave for 24 hours to infuse, then strain. Refrigerate or freeze. MAKES 1 LITRE

100 g carrots

100 g onions

100 g leeks

100 g celery

1 litre water

6 whole white peppercorns

2 star anise

½ lemon, sliced

200 ml dry white wine

Clarified butter

In a heavy-based saucepan, melt the butter over a moderate heat so that the solids and liquid separate. Skim off all the impurities from the top, then strain through a fine sieve, being careful not to pour the milk residue at the bottom of the saucepan into the clarified butter. Clarified butter can be stored for up to five days in the refrigerator, provided it is tightly covered. MAKES 450 ML

500 g unsalted butter

Four citrus beurre blanc

For the citrus mixture, zest the orange and lemon. Juice the orange, lemon, grapefruit and lime and pour the juice into a heavy-based saucepan. Add the onion slices, vinegar and the zest. Place on the stove over medium heat and reduce to a quarter of its original volume. Remove from the heat and stir in the peppercorns.

For the beurre blanc, bring the cream and 50 ml of the citrus mixture to the boil. Add the butter and remove from the heat, whisking continuously until all the butter has emulsified. Do not put back on the heat or the sauce will split. Serve at once. MAKES 120 ML

CITRUS MIXTURE

1 orange

1 lemon

1 grapefruit

1 lime

100 g baby onions, finely sliced

100 ml white wine vinegar

6 whole white peppercorns

BEURRE BLANC

50 ml double cream

50 g butter

Home-made fish seasoning

zest of 1 orange
zest of ½ lemon
100 g dried thyme
4 star anise
500 g coarse sea salt
100 g freshly ground black
   pepper

Place all the ingredients on a tray and leave in a dry, warm place to dry out for two days. Place all the ingredients in a blender and blend until fine. Empty into an airtight container and store for up to six months. MAKES 700 G

Balsamic reduction

500 ml balsamic vinegar

In a pan, bring the balsamic vinegar to the boil and reduce it until large bubbles start to appear. Keep a close eye on it as the sugars in the balsamic vinegar burn very easily. Remove from the heat and cool. The reduction can be stored for up to one month in the refrigerator. MAKES 100 ML

Chilli jam

500 g sugar
250 ml vinegar
2 x 200 ml cans tomato cocktail
100 ml sambal oelek
5 ml grated root ginger

In a heavy-based saucepan over a low heat, dissolve the sugar in the vinegar, stirring now and then. Add the remaining ingredients and cook until thick and syrupy. MAKES 500 ML

Chutney

In a heavy-based saucepan, bring the peaches, apricots and water to the boil, then reduce the heat and simmer until the fruit is soft. Add the onion, garlic and salt. In a separate saucepan, heat the vinegar and sugar until the sugar has dissolved. Add the fruit mixture to the vinegar mixture and continue to simmer until soft. Any other fruit can be added for a different flavour. To thicken the chutney, add some banana. MAKES 1.5 LITRES

200 g peaches, peeled, stoned
   and chopped
250 g apricots, peeled, stoned
   and chopped
500 ml water
1 medium onion, chopped
10 ml crushed garlic
5 ml salt
400 ml brown vinegar
275 g sugar

Tartare sauce

Whisk the egg yolk until light and fluffy, then add the mustard, vinegar and salt. Mix well. Slowly add the oil, whisking continuously until all the oil has been incorporated. Finely chop the onion, capers and cucumber, then mix them into the sauce. Stir in the chopped parsley. MAKES 300 ML

1 egg yolk
5 ml prepared English mustard
10 ml white wine vinegar
5 ml salt
300 ml vegetable oil
½ onion
50 g capers
1 large dill cucumber
a small bunch fresh parsley,
   chopped

Port jus

5 kg beef bones
2 small onions, chopped
2 small leeks, chopped
2 medium carrots, chopped
4 sticks celery, chopped
100 g tomato paste
1 litre red wine
5 litres water
750 ml port
a large handful fresh rosemary
4 bay leaves

Place the beef bones in a roasting pan and roast in a preheated oven at 180 °C until brown, but not burnt. Pour off excess fat. In a large, heavy-based saucepan brown the vegetables in a little sunflower oil. Add the tomato paste and cook for about 6 minutes, then deglaze with half the red wine. Add the bones to the saucepan, cover with water and simmer for 7–8 hours. Skim off the fat and any impurities every 30 minutes. Strain through a fine sieve. In a clean saucepan, reduce the rest of the red wine by half, then add the stock and reduce by half again. Strain. In a separate saucepan, reduce the port by half, then add the stock, rosemary and bay leaves. Reduce to a sauce consistency, then strain again. The jus can be stored in the refrigerator for up to a week, or it can be frozen. MAKES 800 ML

Red wine jus

500 ml red wine
100 ml port
100 g shallots, finely chopped
a sprig fresh thyme
2 litres brown chicken stock
   (see recipe, page 152)
50 g chilled butter

Place the red wine, port, shallots and thyme in a pan. Bring to the boil and reduce by two-thirds. Add the stock and reduce by half. Season and set aside. When needed, bring to the boil, then remove from the heat and enrich with butter, whisking continuously. The jus can be stored for up to a week in the refrigerator. MAKES 1 LITRE

Roast chicken jus

50 ml sunflower oil
400 g chicken bones
1 each onion, carrot and leek
2 sticks celery
30 ml tomato paste
1 clove garlic
1 bay leaf
2 sprigs fresh thyme
300 ml white white
1.5 litres cold water

Place the oil in a roasting pan and heat in a preheated oven at 200 °C for 10 minutes. Add the bones and roast until lightly browned. Chop the onion, carrot, leek and celery and add to the pan. Roast for 15 minutes. Add the tomato paste, garlic and herbs and stir. Roast for 15 minutes more. Add the wine and return to the oven for 5 minutes. Remove from the oven and transfer the pan contents to a large, deep saucepan. Add the water. Bring to the boil as quickly as possible over a high heat. Remove any scum from the surface, reduce the heat and leave to simmer for 4 hours. Strain through a fine sieve, then return to the stove and bring to a rapid boil. Reduce until you have a concentrated jus with a coating consistency. MAKES 500 ML

Duck jus

Place the duck carcasses in a roasting pan and roast in a preheated oven at 180 °C until brown, but not burnt. Pour off excess fat. In a large, heavy-based saucepan brown the vegetables in a little sunflower oil. Add the tomato paste and cook for 5–6 minutes, then deglaze with half the red wine. Add the carcasses to the saucepan, cover with water, add the bay leaves and simmer for 4 hours. Skim off the fat and any impurities every 30 minutes. Strain through a fine sieve. In a clean saucepan, reduce the rest of the wine by half, then add the stock and reduce by half. Strain. In a separate saucepan, reduce the port by half, then add the stock and reduce to a sauce consistency. This jus can be stored in the refrigerator for up to a week, or it can be frozen. MAKES 2 LITRES

5 whole duck carcasses
2 small onions, chopped
2 small leeks, chopped
2 large carrots, chopped
4 sticks celery, chopped
sunflower oil for frying
100 g tomato paste
1.5 litres red wine
5 litres water
4 bay leaves
200 ml port

Thyme jus

Place the lamb bones in a roasting pan and roast in a preheated oven at 180 °C until brown, but not burnt. Pour off any excess fat. In a large, heavy-based saucepan brown the vegetables in a little sunflower oil. Add the tomato paste and cook for a few minutes, then deglaze with half the red wine. Add the bones to the saucepan, cover with water, add the bay leaves and simmer for 5 hours. Skim off the fat and any impurities every 30 minutes. Strain through a fine sieve. In a clean saucepan, reduce the rest of the wine by half, then add the stock and reduce by half. Strain. In a separate saucepan, reduce the port by half, then add the stock and thyme and reduce to a sauce consistency. Strain. The jus can be stored in the refrigerator for up to a week, or it can be frozen. MAKES 800 ML

5 kg lamb bones
2 small onions, chopped
2 small leeks, chopped
2 large carrots, chopped
4 sticks celery, chopped
sunflower oil for frying
100 g tomato paste
1.5 litres red wine
5 litres water
4 bay leaves
200 ml port
a large handful fresh thyme

Velouté

1 small onion, finely chopped

a little sunflower oil

150 ml Chardonnay

700 ml fish stock (see recipe,
   page 152)

200 ml fresh cream

20 ml cold butter, cubed

Sweat the onion in a little oil in a saucepan for a few minutes. Add the wine and reduce by half. Add the fish stock and reduce by half again, then strain through a fine sieve. Return to the heat, add the cream and reduce by half. Whisk in the cold butter. Use immediately. MAKES 400 ML

Sauce verge

3 small shallots, finely chopped

6 coriander seeds, crushed

50 ml olive oil

5 ml lemon juice

2.5 ml balsamic vinegar

6 fresh basil leaves

6 fresh coriander leaves

salt and freshly ground black
   pepper to taste

6 tomatoes, skinned, seeded
   and coarsely chopped

In a saucepan, sauté the shallots and coriander seeds in the olive oil. Add the lemon juice and vinegar. Cook for 5 minutes, then add the herbs and seasoning. Add the chopped tomatoes just before serving. MAKES 60 ML

Red wine vinaigrette

500 ml red wine

100 ml red wine vinegar

150 g sugar

100 ml extra virgin olive oil

In a heavy-based saucepan, heat the red wine and vinegar. Add the sugar and stir to dissolve. Bring to the boil and reduce the liquid to coating consistency. Remove from the heat and leave to cool, then whisk in the olive oil. The vinaigrette can be stored in the refrigerator for up to 15 days. MAKES 500 ML

White wine vinaigrette

Place the vinegars, lemon juice, sugar and seasoning in a bowl. Gradually add the oils, whisking until all the ingredients are combined. Store for up to 15 days in the refrigerator. MAKES 300 ML

50 ml white wine vinegar
30 ml sherry vinegar
30 ml lemon juice
5 ml sugar
salt and freshly ground black
    pepper to taste
100 ml extra virgin olive oil
100 ml canola oil

Basil pesto

Place all the ingredients in a blender and blend until smooth. This pesto can be stored in the refrigerator for up to 15 days. MAKES 500 ML

500 ml olive oil
200 g fresh basil leaves,
    finely chopped
50 g pine nuts, finely chopped
5 ml salt
5 ml freshly ground black
    pepper
25 ml grated Parmesan
3 cloves garlic, chopped

Coriander pesto

Place all the ingredients, except the oil, in a blender. Switch it on and, with the motor running, slowly add the oil and blend until smooth. MAKES 200 ML

250 ml fresh coriander,
    chopped
125 ml fresh parsley, chopped
80 g cashew nuts
½ clove garlic
12.5 ml grated Parmesan
200 ml canola oil

Potato rosti

4 large potatoes, peeled
100 g clarified butter
  (see recipe, page 153)
a sprig fresh thyme
5 ml salt
a pinch of freshly ground
  black pepper

Grate the potatoes onto a clean kitchen towel, then gather up the corners of the towel and squeeze out the excess water. Place the grated potatoes in a bowl with half the clarified butter, and the thyme leaves and seasoning. Mix together. Lightly grease a small frying pan with some clarified butter and place a quarter of the potato mixture into the pan. Pack tightly. Fry gently until golden brown, then turn and fry the other side. Add some more clarified butter and repeat the process with the remaining potato. MAKES 4 ROSTIS

Saffron potato cakes

250 g butter
4 strands saffron
6 medium potatoes, peeled
salt to taste

Melt the butter over a low heat. Remove from the heat and add the saffron. Leave to infuse for 2 hours. Cut the potatoes into equal sized pieces and place in a saucepan. Cover with water, bring to the boil and cook until just soft. Drain the potatoes and place in a perforated aluminium foil roasting pan. Roast in a preheated oven at 180 °C for 10 minutes. Mix the potatoes with the saffron butter and season. Spoon 150 g of potato mix into each ring mould and press down firmly. Reheat in the oven for a few minutes. MAKES 6 CAKES

Lasagne sheets

600 g cake flour
4 eggs
6 egg yolks
10 ml salt
30 ml fresh cream
30 ml olive oil

Place the flour in a food processor. Add the eggs and yolks one at a time, using the pulse setting to mix them into the flour. Add the salt, cream and olive oil and continue to pulse. The mixture should bind together like a ball of dough. Remove the dough from the machine and knead on a lightly floured surface. Cut into five equal-sized pieces, then wrap in clingfilm and place in the refrigerator for at least 1 hour to rest. Using a pasta machine, roll the dough to a thickness of 1.5 mm. Cut the dough into 6 cm diameter discs with a pastry cutter. To freeze, layer the sheets with clingfilm in between and cover tightly with more clingfilm. MAKES 600 G (ABOUT 50 SHEETS)

Baby carrot/onion confit

Peel and wash the carrots or onions. Place all the ingredients on aluminium foil and wrap up into a tight parcel. Place in a preheated oven at 180 °C for about 10 minutes. Remove from the oven and set aside for later use. SERVES 6

24 baby carrots or baby onions

a sprig fresh thyme

1 clove garlic

5 ml coarse sea salt

a pinch of freshly ground
  black pepper

15 ml olive oil

Tomato salsa

Blanch the tomatoes in boiling water for 20–30 seconds, then plunge into ice water. Peel off the skin, cut into quarters and remove the seeds. Finely dice the tomato flesh. Finely chop the spring onions. Toast the sesame seeds under the grill until golden brown. Mix together the tomatoes, spring onions, sesame seeds and vinegar and season. MAKES 500 G

6 tomatoes

2 spring onions

5 ml sesame seeds

15 ml red wine vinegar

salt and freshly ground black
  pepper to taste

Sweet pastry tartlet cases

Cream the butter and sugar. Add 1 of the eggs and mix well. Sift the flour and allspice and add to the creamed mixture. Mix well, but be careful not to overmix. Wrap the pastry in clingfilm and set aside for 30 minutes in the refrigerator. On a floured surface, roll out the pastry to 2 mm thick, then line buttered tart moulds with the pastry. Line the pastry moulds with greaseproof paper and fill with dried beans or lentils. Bake in a preheated oven at 180 °C for 10 minutes. Remove and discard the beans and paper and bake for 8 minutes more. Whisk together the remaining egg and the milk and lightly brush the tart cases with the mixture. Bake for 5 minutes. Remove and set aside until needed. MAKES 4

250 g butter

125 g sugar

2 eggs

375 g cake flour

a pinch of ground allspice

20 ml milk

Strawberry coulis

Place all the ingredients in a blender and blend until smooth. Pass through a fine sieve and refrigerate until needed. MAKES 400 ML

300 g strawberries

100 g sugar

20 ml lemon juice

Crème anglaise

250 ml milk
250 ml fresh cream
¼ vanilla pod
6 egg yolks
75 g sugar

In a heavy-based saucepan, heat the milk and cream, together with the vanilla pod, but don't let it boil. Strain through a fine sieve. In a mixing bowl, whisk together the egg yolks and sugar until light and fluffy. Mix a little of the warm milk into the egg mixture, then add the egg mixture to the milk and cook in a double-boiler until the custard is thick and smooth, whisking constantly. Strain through a fine sieve. MAKES 500 ML

Crème pâtissière

500 ml milk
5 ml vanilla essence
100 g castor sugar
6 egg yolks
70 ml cake flour
30 ml cornflour

In a saucepan, bring the milk and vanilla essence to the boil, then remove from the heat and set aside. Whisk together the sugar and egg yolks until pale, then add the flour and cornflour. Slowly add the hot milk to the egg mixture and mix thoroughly. Return the mixture to the saucepan and slowly bring to the boil, stirring constantly until thick. Remove from the heat and cool. MAKES 500 ML

Tuile baskets

7 egg whites
250 g cake flour
200 g icing sugar
175 g butter, melted
5 ml vanilla essence

Whisk the egg whites until soft peaks form, then fold in the flour and icing sugar. Fold in the melted butter and vanilla essence until well combined. Shape into baskets (or other desired shape), then leave to rest in the refrigerator for about 2 hours before use. MAKES 6 SMALL BASKETS

Chocolate sauce

200 ml fresh cream
150 g dark Callebaut Belgian
    chocolate, broken into
    small pieces
10 ml orange liqueur
    (Cointreaux or
    Grand Marnier)

Slowly bring the cream to the boil, then remove from the heat and stir in the chocolate until melted. Stir in the liqueur. MAKES 300 ML

Index

Accompaniments
Bread, flowerpot 140
Chilli jam 154
Chilli and lime sorbet 98
Chutney 155
Crêpes 70, 124
Fish seasoning, home-
made 154
Lasagne sheets 160
Parmesan crisps 99
Pesto, Basil 159
Coriander 69, 159
Polenta chips 138
Tomato salsa 29

**Batters, Butters, Stocks
and Gravies**
Batter, Crêpe 124
Tempura 79
Butter, Clarified 153
Herbed 70
Peppadew 143
Jus, Duck 157
Port 156
Red wine 156
Roast chicken 156
Thyme 157
Truffle-scented 86
Marinade, quail 74
Oil, red pepper 70
Stock, Chicken 152
Fish 152
Vegetable 153

Beef
Bobotie 50
Roast fillet 30
with cabbage parcels,
sweet potato fondant,
asparagus and bone
marrow 105

Creams and Sauces (Savoury)
Balsamic reduction 154
Beurre blanc, four citrus 153
Cream, Basil 26
Truffle 20
Watercress 115
Foam, Basil 97
Rocket 138
Sauces, Tartare 155
Tomato 82
Verge 158
Vierge base 34
Velouté 158
Purée, herb 33

Creams and Sauces (Sweet)
Balsamic syrup 126
Crème anglaise 96, 162
Crème pâtissière 88, 162
Custard 40
Mint cream 124
Raspberry sabayon 95
Sauces, Brandy 117
Chocolate 162
Malva pudding 60
Strawberry coulis 161

Desserts
Biscotti, chocolate and
mixed nut 118
Biscuits, hazelnut 95
Boeber 64
Chocolate, Marquise with a
raspberry sabayon and
hazelnut biscuits 95
Plate 'Liz McGrath' 38
Tart with chocolate
sorbet 92
Coffee crème brûlée with
chocolate and mixed
nut biscotti 118

Crème brûlée 147
Coffee 118
Date and chocolate
pudding with mocha
ice cream 123
Date pudding with
rum-and-raisin ice
cream and sweet
potato spaghetti 90–91
Floating island 40
Ice cream, Balsamic 124
Cheesecake 148
Mocha 123
Rum-and-raisin 90
Vanilla yoghurt 120
White chocolate 39
Jelly, Mango 96
Passion fruit 96
Raspberry 96
Koeksisters 63
Malva pudding 60
Milk tart 61
Parfait, Dark chocolate-raisin
with brandy sauce 117
Wild honey with fresh
strawberries in balsamic
syrup 126
Passion fruit chiboust 88
Raspberry shortcake with
cheesecake ice cream 148
Sorbet, Chocolate 92
Lemon 150
Melon 150
Orange 150
Soufflé, Passion fruit 37
Raspberry and peach 120
Stawberry tart 36
Sweet pastry tartlet case 161
Tart, Chocolate 92
Milk 61
Strawberry 36, 124

Strawberries with mint
cream and balsamic ice
cream, 'torta' 124
Jellies, trio of fruit, with
crème anglaise 96
Sorbets, trio of summer 150
Tuile baskets 162

Dressings
Balsamic 28
Caesar salad 135
Honey and soy 25
Lemon-paprika 69
Orange 74
Vinaigrette, White wine 59
Mustard 22
Red wine 74, 158
Ruby port 72
Seafood 132

Fish and Seafood
Bobotie, fish 46
Bunny chow 140–141
Calamari, stir-fried 142
Crayfish, grilled with
peppadew butter,
sautéed baby potatoes
and roasted
asparagus 143
Fish and chips, rich man's 136
Fish cakes, traditional 131
Kabeljou, grilled with saffron
potato cakes and tomato
confit, served with a
langoustine and
chardonnay velouté 102
Kingklip, roasted with a
crisp salmon and lemon
grass risotto cake and
cucumber spaghetti
with wasabi dressing 76

Line fish with red pepper sauce, polenta chips, ratatouille and rocket foam 138

Mussel and red pepper charlotte 70

Mussels in Cape Malay broth 65

Oysters, fresh Knysna with a chilli and lime sorbet 98

Prawns and avocado with tomato salsa 29

Prawns and creamed leeks, ravioli of 132

Prawns, seared in a lemon-paprika dressing on a cracked wheat salad with coriander pesto 69

Prawns, tiger, grilled with stir-fried vegetables 144

Salmon, pan fried Cape, braised cucumber, roasted fennel, pommes aux crasse and basil cream 26

Salmon, smoked, with deep-fried oysters and four citrus beurre blanc 23

Salmon, smoked, wrapped in steamed butter lettuce 66

Seafood soup, Marine 130

Snoek soup 44

Snoek, traditional smoor 45

Sole, grilled Walker Bay 137

Sole, grilled with creamed leeks, mashed potato and tempura calamari scented with lemon 79

Yellowtail niçoise, grilled 28

Lamb

Bredie, tomato 52

Denningvleis 51

Loin, pan-fried, dauphinoise potatoes, roast garlic and onions and portabellini mushrooms with a thyme jus 106

Rack, hay-roasted 33 with ratatouille and crushed potatoes with chevin 82

Pasta

Lasagne, summer garden 115

Ravioli of prawns and creamed leeks 132

Gorgonzola 72

Pork

Cutlets, grilled, with bean and corn ragout, and sage and apple compote 80

Poultry

Chicken, Biryani 55

Breast, grilled with batons of polenta chips and truffle-scented jus 86

Livers 'peri-peri' 49

Pie 56

Salad, sesame with honey and soy dressing 25

Roast breast on a basil and tomato tart 112

Warm liver parfait served with gorgonzola ravioli and a ruby port vinaigrette 72–73

Duck, slow-roasted leg with sesame and orange, and pan-seared breast, with basmati rice and stir-fried vegetables 108

Ostrich, roast tandoori-spiced fillet 110

Carpaccio, with a mille-fuelle of rocket and Parmesan, served with a red wine vinaigrette 99

Quail, deboned marinated in red wine and marmalade with a warm beetroot salad and orange dressing 74

Soups

Butternut soup 17

Cauliflower and mushroom soup 19

Mussels in Cape Malay broth 65

Roast tomato and ratatouille soup with basil foam 97

Snoek soup 44

Vegetables and Salads

Asparagus, green and truffle cream 20

Butternut, roasted and Saint-Maure mille-feuille, garden herb salad and sauce vierge 34

Carrot/onion confit, baby 161

Chickpea and lentil curry 57

Dahl curry 58

Goat's cheese, deep-fried, French bean salad and mustard vinaigrette 22

Lasagne, summer garden 115

Potato cakes, saffron 160

Potato rosti 160

Tomato salsa 161

Vegetable terrine with pesto, Mediterranean 100

Venison

Springbok loin, oven-roasted, with onion, sultana and garlic compote 85

CONVERSION TABLE		
METRIC	US CUPS	IMPERIAL
5 ml	1 tsp	3/16 fl oz
15 ml	1 Tbsp	1/2 fl oz
60 ml	4 Tbsp/1/4 cup	2 fl oz
80 ml	1/3 cup	2 3/4 fl oz
125 ml	1/2 cup	4 1/2 fl oz
160 ml	2/3 cup	5 1/2 fl oz
200 ml	3/4 cup	7 fl oz
250 ml	1 cup	9 fl oz
100 g	–	3 1/2 oz
250 g	–	9 oz
500 g	–	1 lb
750 g	–	1 3/4 lb
1 kg	–	2 1/4 lb